TREES, SHRUBS, AND ROSES

FOR MIDWEST GARDENS

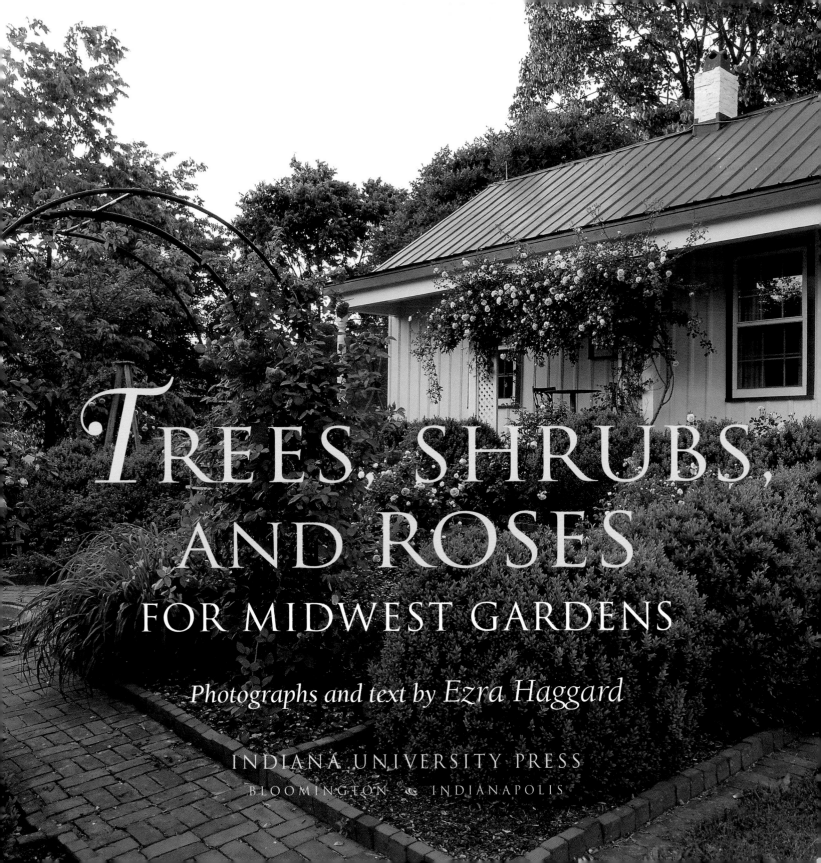

TREES, SHRUBS, AND ROSES
FOR MIDWEST GARDENS

Photographs and text by Ezra Haggard

INDIANA UNIVERSITY PRESS

BLOOMINGTON ❦ INDIANAPOLIS

This book is a publication of

Indiana University Press
601 North Morton Street
Bloomington, Indiana 47404-3797 USA

http://iupress.indiana.edu

Telephone orders   800-842-6796
Fax orders   812-855-7931
Orders by e-mail   iuporder@indiana.edu

The paper used in this publication meets the
minimum requirements of American National
Standard for Information Sciences—Permanence
of Paper for Printed Library Materials,
ANSI Z39.48–1984.

Manufactured in Singapore

Library of Congress Cataloging-in-Publication Data

Haggard, Ezra.
   Trees, shrubs, and roses for midwest gardens /
 photographs and text by Ezra Haggard.
        p.   cm.
   Includes bibliographical references (p.   ).
   ISBN 0-253-33961-8 (cl : alk. paper) — ISBN 0-253-21470-X
 (pa : alk. paper)
    1. Ornamental trees—Middle West. 2. Ornamental shrubs—
 Middle West. 3. Roses—Middle West. I. Title.
 SB435.52.M5 H35 2001
 635.9'77'0978—dc21
                                        00-143856

 1 2   3 4 5 06 05 04 03 02 01

This book is dedicated to Ms. Peel, who loved to climb trees.

Contents

Acknowledgments

I first have to thank Dr. Willem Meijer from the School of Biological Sciences at the University of Kentucky. I developed my appreciation for trees in his dendrology course, as we tromped around the woods learning to identify native trees with the aid of his book, *Tree Flora of Kentucky*. I also learned a lot from Michael Dirr, J. W. and Jim Singer, and Donald Wyman.

I next want to thank everyone who in the past two years willingly shared their time and knowledge whenever I called with a question, and everyone who allowed me into their garden to photograph. You are too numerous to mention, but I am deeply grateful to all of you. Special thanks go to the Chicago Botanic Garden, the Missouri Botanical Garden, and the University of Kentucky Arboretum.

I could not have completed the book without the help of editor Bobbi Diehl. I owe endless gratitude to the other wonderful people at Indiana University Press, friend and plantsman Tim Morehouse, and tree enthusiasts Rick Fredrick and Richard Weber. Thanks also go to Paul Cappiello, Louie Hillenmeyer, Bob Klausing, Helen Kruse, John Michler, Ted Potter, Brian Jorg and Mat Vehr of Spring Grove Cemetery in Cincinnati, Bill Fountain in the Horticulture Department at the University of Kentucky, and Marsha Farris at the U.K. Arboretum, for sharing their knowledge and time.

Special thanks to Dana Corman for her unfailing support and encouragement.

A bold Japanese lantern nestled among azaleas with red Japanese maples in the background.

Introduction

The purpose of this book is to demonstrate how to use trees, shrubs, and roses effectively. That this is a subject in need of demystification becomes clear from a survey of just about any midwestern yard at just about any time of year. With its expanse of lawn, its obligatory "ornamental" tree right in the center, yews or junipers girdling the house, and possibly a forsythia or burning bush plopped down in a corner, it is unimaginative, to say the least. Yet one also sees some exceptions to this rule: yards that *don't* look like everyone else's, where the gardeners have been having some fun and expressing their individuality, where gardening is a rewarding hobby and an ongoing process. If you are in the latter group, or want to be, this book will help you take things a step or two further by teaching you some of the principles of landscape design, acquainting you with some previously unfamiliar plants that you may want to add to your personal landscape, and suggesting appropriate companion plants.

These trees, shrubs, and roses are, I feel, some of the best ornamentals for the middle part of the North American continent. I have used them time and again in gardens that I have designed and developed. All are reliable. All have appeal for more than one season. Virtually all are hardy in Zones 5 and 6 (and if not, it is noted); some are also hardy farther north, and some will do well farther south. Some are readily available; others will take some detective work to locate.

In addition to being valuable sources of planting ideas, midwestern botanical gardens and arboretums will help you find retail sources for trees, shrubs, and other plants. If your local nursery does not have the plants you desire and is not willing to special order (most are), there are probably landscape professionals in your area who can obtain them from wholesale sources. Mail order nurseries, especially those in the Midwest, are an excellent resource, although their stock may need growing on for a year or two. Last but not least, many a gardener has stumbled upon an unusual plant bargain at Target, K-Mart, Home Depot, or Lowe's. You never know what may turn up in the garden departments of these big stores.

Usually gardeners select a shrub or tree on the basis of looks. We are tempted by an attractive plant, and we take it home and look for a place to put it. This can work out satisfactorily, but usually the plant is placed where it soon outgrows the space or encroaches on nearby plants. It is better to determine the spot first, and then choose something that will fit there both culturally and spatially. As Jens Jensen remarks in *Siftings*, you should "find the plant which need not be maimed and distorted to fit the situation. Every plant has its fitness and must be placed in its proper surround[ing]s so as to bring out its beauty." Choosing the right tree or shrub for the location will mean less work and expense in the long run. No pruning, trimming, or removal need ever be done if the tree or shrub is sited properly and its cultural requirements are taken care of.

The best gardens do not necessarily reflect the latest fads, hot ideas, and popular plants, but they should reflect the natural plant community: a grouping of trees, shrubs, and perennials, just as is found in nature.

Trees always come to mind first because of their stature. The visual image they evoke tells us how to use them, individually and as part of a garden or landscape. Trees add height in the garden. They frame, anchor, and connect all the elements to the sky. Take the photograph of the 'Red Cloud' dogwood (*Cornus florida*), for example. By means of its height, the tree ties the house in the background to the garden in the front. At the same time, it links the garden to the sky. Without the tree in the scene, the garden would be flat. The eye could take it all in at once, without pausing to appreciate its features.

The trees in the book were chosen for their ornamental value not only at bloom time but year round. Characteristics that extend the ornamental value can include the color or shape of the foliage (goldenrain tree); unique, dappled bark (riverbirch, lacebark elm); and form (amur and hedge maples). Additionally, my choices stay relatively small—no more than 30–35' (with a very few exceptions, such as the katsuratree)—in order to maintain scale for most home and garden spaces.

Since shrubs are almost limitless in their variety, easy to care for, and usually fairly fast growing, a lot can be accomplished with them. They also add another structural element, visually softening the trees, connecting them to a larger landscape. The photograph of bottlebrush buckeye (*Aesculus parviflora*) is an example. Here, taller trees blend in with the boxwood and the bottlebrush. The shrubs soften the vertical element and extend the planting into the larger landscape.

Both trees and shrubs work together structurally (in terms of size and shape) while adding color and texture. If more drama is needed to emphasize a view, a bolder contrast of color can be used. The photograph of *Acer palmatum* 'Bloodgood' illustrates this idea. Color, structure, and texture are all at play here, and the red of 'Bloodgood' is a contrasting element, dramatizing what would otherwise have been a subtle blend of greens. Visually, the color directs the view. To the left, the boxwood touches the tree, connecting it to the rest of the planting, the stones, and the water. Together they all create a larger landscape.

Everyone loves roses, but they are notoriously difficult in the Midwest, particularly the Lower Midwest with its hot and humid summers. Over the years, however, I have learned about a few roses that are easy to care for, and I share them in this book. Their shortcomings as well as their strengths are noted. You will find no hybrid teas here. My favorite roses are vigorous, disease resistant, require little pruning, endure for many years, and of course are beautiful. Being highly individual, they can play a number of roles in the landscape.

So that is what this book is about. Space and time have limited the number of photographs and the amount of advice I could provide, but I have always attempted to explain why each plant was used in a particular situation.

Trees and shrubs define the garden and the landscape more than any other element that we use. Their importance goes far beyond the focus of ornamental value into the realms of healing and spirituality. Our lives are better for their presence, and I hope with this book to encourage gardeners to plant more of them.

TREES, SHRUBS, AND ROSES

FOR MIDWEST GARDENS

Maples

Removing a tree that has outgrown its space is an all too common occurrence—and an expensive one. Throughout the Midwest and Upper South, maples are often planted because they are readily available and cheap. More often than not, these "generic maples" become huge trees in twenty or thirty years, shading everything in their path. Most obnoxious of all, dividing the yard into sections with its surface roots, is the silver maple, which belongs only in its natural element, meaning nowhere within fifty miles of any city. What was a good, economical idea, innocently conceived, soon becomes a very real problem for the lawn mower—and for anything trying to grow beneath its canopy. Dealing with huge, unwanted trees has been a career-long challenge for me.

Your life can be easier, and you can have maples aplenty, with a little effort and careful selection. The eight trees described below are included for their importance in defining smaller spaces, and can be used individually or collectively. Although some have bright colored, winged seeds (samaras) that are attractive, none have a drop-dead flower display. But they are ornamental in other important ways, for they possess a range of attributes that are indispensable for creating gardens and landscapes. All are under 40' tall. All have neat, rounded outlines. Varied shape and foliage texture among the group provides endless combinations. All have unique characteristics for solving structural and ornamental problems. It may take a little detective work to find some of these trees, but I guarantee that you will not regret the effort.

Opposite: Green and red *dissectum* Japanese maples with daffodils, liriope, and Korean boxwood hedging create a driveway island.

The trident maple
with its mottled bark,
underplanted with
caladiums, ferns,
and houttuynia.

The small, well-rounded trident maple deserves to be more widely available. Topping out at 25 to 35', with low branching and multi-stemmed habit, it is wonderfully versatile. The multiple branches support a tightly rounded or oval crown of dark green foliage. Over time, the excellence of this tree becomes apparent despite its handicap of having no blossoms to impress with. It is useful and handsome, slow in growth, unrivaled for its colorful, textured bark, and hardy to Zone 5.

The flowers are hardly noticeable, but the foliage is small, dark green, from $1^{1}/_{2}$ to $3^{1}/_{2}$", looking like green duck feet, with three distinct lobes that give the maple its name. Another bonus with this maple is its show of color in late October to early November, when the foliage turns deep yellow, orange, and dark red. With age, the bark ripens and separates into vertical plates that curl and peel away from the trunk, exposing a soft orange underneath.

Tough and adaptable, the trident maple can withstand extremes of heat and cold, go through a drought without leaf scorching, and thrive in infertile soil. It transplants easily, whether balled and burlapped or in a container. I have moved it successfully in full foliage from a container. Well-drained soil is a must. The tree in the photograph is growing in clay soil that drains well. It does best in full sun; seen here facing west, it does well enough.

This is a great tree for small spaces, under utility lines, placed where a screen is needed, for maintaining scale with other features, and to add height. Several could be used in planters on a patio, or to frame an entrance. Limbed up, the trident maple is an asset close to a house that will give an unobstructed view and plenty of light for a complementary planting underneath.

Acer buergerianum
(a-ser ber-jar-e-a'num)
TRIDENT MAPLE

Touched by morning light, hedge maple between companions of butterfly bush and hydrangea.

Like the trident maple, *Acer campestre* is a useful, short tree. It is difficult to get excited about it until you learn about its durability and handsome structure. The foliage is the most interesting characteristic, forming a well-rounded crown and dense branches. The hedge maple is hardier than the trident, making it easier to use in the upper regions of the Midwest.

Its name derives from the fact that it is frequently found in English hedgerows. It follows that this maple takes well to pruning. With a low branching habit and a 25 to 35' height and width, *campestre* is ideal hedge and screening material. I tend to shy away from obsessive clipping of trees and shrubs if there is any other way to get a similar effect. In a garden situation it looks more natural with branches all the way to the ground. As a single specimen, it can be limbed up so that light can penetrate the dense branches.

When I first laid eyes on *Acer campestre,* my thought was that its leaves resemble those of a miniature maple. The foliage is only 2 to 4" in length and width, deeply lobed and rounded, with a smooth, dark green topside and a hairy underside. The fall color is nothing to applaud, but there is a greenish-yellow to yellow color that is satisfying. As the tree ages, branches can be really attractive, with corky fissures running up the bark. A slow grower, it offers many advantages for the garden.

This is a tough tree, adaptable to both sweet and acidic soils, and tolerant of dry soils. One of its best characteristics is its ability to withstand compacted soils, such as at newly constructed home sites. *A. campestre* will perform under adverse conditions, in sun or light shade, but prefers rich well-drained soil.

There are other situations for which the hedge maple is ideal. Try it in light shade under an older tree, to screen an adjacent area that the older tree no longer hides. The height is good for small properties and gardens and under utility lines. Limbed up, the hedge maple would be compatible with shade perennials. *A. c.* 'Queen Elizabeth' ('Evelyn') is an especially vigorous cultivar. Either one would be a good choice for a large box planter.

Acer campestre
(a'ser kam-pes'tre)
HEDGE MAPLE

Two amur maples
create a frame for
oakleaf hydrangea
and *Iris pseudacorus*.

How could maples get any better? *Acer ginnala* is easier to find in nurseries than the two previous maples, is hardier, and does better in the shade. Add to that its flowers, fruit, and fall foliage and you have a tree of great value. Now, if even more nurseries would stock them, everyone could discover the wonder of this little tree. Its performance in the shade alone makes this maple worth locating. Hardiness to Zone 2 is another plus. Shorter than the previous two maples, it is usually described as a tall shrub or a small tree. Mature height usually runs between 15–18', sometimes reaching 25'— a useful height for the garden. Older trees have rounded crowns as wide as tall, supported with a smooth trunk of multiple stems.

Flowers, fruit, and fall foliage make this an attractive tree for all seasons. The creamy white flower clusters appear in April and May as the foliage begins to unfurl. The flowers are mildly fragrant, and after they are finished, the typical winged seeds can turn bright brick red in August and September. Leaf color is shiny green in the summer, turning to shades of yellow to dark red in the fall.

Whether B&B or from a container, transplanting is easy. Like the hedge maple, the amur can stand heavy pruning, is adaptable in sweet or acidic soil, and tolerates different soil types. In moist, well-drained soils and a sunny location, it will reward you with maximum growth. It will tolerate light shade under a taller tree, an extended roof line, or in an eastern location.

Amur maple's size makes it versatile. Under a mature and limbed-up specimen would be a perfect place for a bench. Underneath, you can grow lawn or put in shade-loving perennials. This is a good tree with which to screen adjacent properties. From ground level it would conceal without totally shading a small garden. As a centrally located specimen it would be visually prominent without obscuring other features. Planted as a front yard tree, it would not grow out of scale. A focal attraction can be created by limbing up the tree to reveal the smooth bark and branching characteristics. An ideal situation for showing off its shape would be as the central figure within a circular drive, anchored to either side with shrubs and perennials. This would create a beautifully balanced garden while providing privacy from the street.

Acer ginnala
(a'ser jin-na'-la)
AMUR MAPLE

Electric cinnamon
colored bark of
paperbark maple.

If there is such a thing as a darling maple, it is *Acer griseum*. Because it is so desirable, paperbark maple is more readily available than the previous three maples. Its flamboyant, peeling red bark is uniquely attractive year-round. It is vigorous in various soil types and overall an undemanding tree. As long as there is good drainage, it will thrive in Zones 5-8.

With a vertical stature and a rounded crown, the paperbark usually reaches 20 to 30', typically taller than wide. It has an excellent structural form, rising from a single trunk into several major branches, with maturity giving rise to smaller branches up to the height of the tree. The effect is of a perfectly balanced tree.

Distinctively segmented leaves show some blue blended with the dark green and are divided into three unconnected parts. The foliage turns a bright red in the fall, given a good season. Paperbark is one of the last trees to turn color, the leaves sometimes hanging on till November.

Garden writers rave about the spectacular bark. It displays a rich, shiny, reddish brown color that darkens and begins peeling with age. In the second or third year the bark begins to curl outward, peeling away from the trunk, flaking and rolling up at the edges. This characteristic is usually displayed to some extent even on three-year-old trees.

This maple takes full sun, does best in moist, well-drained soils, and tolerates different soil types and pH levels. Its willingness to grow in clay is probably one of its best attributes. Spring is the best time for transplanting. Most of the plants I find in nurseries are in containers.

Paperbarks deserve a prominent place in the garden. I suggest using one by the drive entrance, pruned up to accommodate an understory planting around its base. This will enhance the entrance scene all year. Some interesting perennial companions would be epimedium, autumn fern, and Japanese painted fern. Blue hostas would look fine too. For complementary shrubs, try boxwood, hydrangea, hollies, and rhododendron.

Acer griseum

(a'ser gris'e-um)

PAPERBARK MAPLE

The elegance of
green Japanese maple
contrasted with the red
of 'Bloodgood' maple
and azaleas.

Japanese maples are the aristocrats of the tree world. Their fine texture and beautiful bark have earned them an exalted place in the garden. Their appearance varies, and they have different uses. In the following four essays I have separated out the smaller, shorter ones from the taller.

The species, *palmatum* (Zones 5-8) is a fine-leafed tree. The leaf itself is green, the trunk is also green, and the tree's form is upright. Known in the nursery trade as Green Japanese Maple, it grows slowly up to 15–25' under cultivation, usually with a single trunk and a layering branching habit that enhances its delicacy. Densely branched, the crown forms a round shape, usually as wide as it is tall.

The foliage and bark texture more than make up for the lack of colorful flowers. Foliage emerges a refreshing chartreuse in the spring, turning a bright medium green as it matures and then a lovely golden-yellow in the fall. The leaves are on the small side—2 to 5"—deeply lobed, serrated, and separated into 5 to 7 lobes. On older trees, the bark of the trunk and branches turns a smooth gray but retains some of the green color.

I've had success transplanting the green Japanese maple in balled and burlapped forms or in containers. If there is difficulty getting the plant out of a container, use sharp pruners to make vertical cuts down the sides, then across the bottom from drain-hole to drain-hole, disturbing the roots as little as possible. I would caution you not to place them out until after all danger of frost is past, but give them an entire growing season to acclimate. Windy positions need to be avoided. Dappled shade is preferred to hot sun and dry soil in the Midwest, although I have had success with them in direct sun when there was good moisture and well-drained soil.

During the early spring freezes of 1997 and 2000 the green Japanese maple came through with hardly any leaf damage compared to the *dissectum* cultivars. But those were the only two years in the past thirty that Japanese maples suffered any setback at all in our area.

Use green Japanese maples where there is a need for a soft, vertical presence. Try one planted poolside, limbed up to allow companions of azalea, bergenia, and a small 'Bloodgood'.

Acer palmatum

(a'ser pal-ma' tum)

GREEN JAPANESE MAPLE

'Bloodgood' Japanese maple, enhancing the view with boxwood and pine, at the Japanese Garden, Missouri Botanical Garden.

Over the years, this has usually been the tree most people visualize when they think about Japanese maples. It lends a graceful and exotic effect, its red foliage and fine texture making a welcome interruption to a predominantly green landscape. Factoring in its small size, adaptability, and undemanding nature, 'Bloodgood' is a useful tree indeed. 'Moonfire', another *atropurpureum* cultivar, is also good. These are the two I've planted the most.

Broadly round-headed, the crown spreads out more horizontally than vertically, giving this tree an inverted pyramid shape that adds to its gracefulness. Eventual height is around 15', with a broader width, after approximately 15 years. It does grow slowly but is well worth the wait, and while waiting one can enjoy the foliage color.

The main attraction of this small tree is its delicate foliage. Small and deeply lobed, it is finely serrated and has a flat burgundy or reddish-purple hue. The leaves hang, pointed downward, as if floating in the air rather than being fastened to a stem. 'Bloodgood' retains its color in the grueling heat of Lower Midwest/Upper South summers. Fall turns the foliage an electric crimson.

They like the same soil conditions as the green Japanese maple and are equally adaptable. Plant in full sun and moist soil for best growth. To retain soil moisture, a liberal application of pine bark mini-nugget mulch should be maintained. They seem to grow faster and have richer foliage in dappled shade, but if kept mulched, with adequate moisture, they will do well in sun.

As a design strategy, the placement of red maples in the photo creates a layering contrast with sky, rock, and water. The colorful separations are meant to be appreciated from below, looking up to the waterfall.

The use of this tree is only restrained by the imagination. 'Bloodgood' can add a Japanese look to the garden, especially if limbed up to accentuate the sculptural twisting of the branches. Planted in an eminently visible spot, such as hanging over an ornamental pool, it connects pool to sky. The red foliage is striking reflected in a swimming pool, too. Either type of reflection will create a peaceful view. It is a tree small enough to be used in any prominent position—under taller trees, limbed up so that short perennials like the Japanese painted fern, *Astilbe chinensis* 'Pumila', any ajuga, or annuals such as pink and white impatiens can reside underneath.

Acer palmatum var. *atropurpureum* 'Bloodgood'

BLOODGOOD
JAPANESE MAPLE

Red and green laceleafs among white azaleas, lining the stream and extending the perspective to a centrally featured magnolia. The pendulous characteristic of the *dissectums* is ready-made for a water feature; there is a Japanese "style" inherent in using this tree. Here, the delicate leaves of 'Crimson Queen' also make a foil for the hard, gray granite.

The *dissectum* group of Japanese maples resemble weeping ferns. *Acer palmatum* var. *dissectum* 'Crimson Queen' delights from spring through fall and serves as a natural sculpture in winter. Foliage, form, and structure all combine to make it one of the most interesting trees for the garden. 'Crimson Queen' (and others in this group, such as 'Garnet') tend to form shrubby mounds, wider than tall, 8' to 10' in height and 12' wide. Branches can be kept weeping all the way to the ground or be pruned up for a more tree-like, pendulous effect. The gnarled, twisted branches have their own beautiful pattern, creating a triangular shape that takes a while to come into its own. They are hardy to Zones 5 or 6, but should receive extra protection in Zone 5.

The foliage of 'Crimson Queen' is a deep reddish-purple, 5 to 9 lobes deeply cut and finely serrated, delicate and elegant. The red color continues throughout our intense summers, turning a shocking orange in autumn. The intensity of fall color on a mature plant is unsurpassed.

As the tree matures, the branches form a living sculpture, spreading outward and curving upward. Adding to the effect, the dark, rich, brownish-black bark is riddled with white rivulets running along the surface.

Although this tree looks refined, it is not culturally delicate, except that it can be damaged by frost. The *dissectums* suffer more from a late frost than the plain *palmatums*. In a late spring 1997 freeze in Lexington, complete dieback occurred. However, with pruning, two seasons later the tree was back to full form. They prefer highly organic soils in dappled shade, although I have had success in less hospitable soil and in full sun with even moisture. Good drainage is essential. Again, they will not tolerate windy sites.

They are easily transplanted from a nursery container of any size up to a 3 x 3' wooden box planter, ready to create an instant feature. I have had one specimen growing for twelve years in good topsoil mounded on top of a clay base soil that drains well. Since moisture is important for this tree, use a generous 4–6" of pine straw or fine pine bark mulch. *Dissectums* are sold in nurseries in huge specimen containers and can continue to survive in them if well protected throughout the winter in the colder parts of the Midwest.

Acer palmatum var. *dissectum* 'Crimson Queen'

RED LACELEAF
JAPANESE MAPLE

Graceful green laceleaf with azaleas in the Missouri Botanical Garden.
You could base a mixed group of Japanese maples either on size or leaf color.
Try 'Bloodgood', 'Moonfire', and 'Crimson Queen' for reds, or use only greens,
or mix greens and reds together. There are no rules.

Many cultivars of the *dissectum* group—red, green, and variegated wonders—are listed in the best reference of all time, J. D. Vertrees' *Japanese Maples* (Timber Press), now in its second edition. This book has been my authority and guide since it was first published. 'Viridis' is treated separately from the reds, used when a delicate green is called for. This green cultivar is even more fern-like, and without the distraction of color the delicate character seems even more pronounced.

The shape of *A. p.* var. *dissectum* 'Viridis' has a more horizontal emphasis than 'Crimson Queen' or the other reds, which are more weeping. 'Viridis' rises from a stout trunk of variable height before beginning the horizontal branching. With a little constructive pruning, this structure lends itself to a "bonsai" effect. Other times I have used it almost like a ground cover, finding a plant with a short trunk and doing no lower limb removal.

Foliage is the best asset of 'Viridis', the color varying from individual to individual. (The name 'Viridis' tends to be a favorite repository for all green-leafed *dissectums*.) The leaves first come out as yellow-green, bright, and tender. As they unfold they show a bronzing along the margin, which fades as the leaf matures but does not disappear entirely. Deep dissecting and divisions create the delicacy of the fern-like foliage. With the green laceleaf, fall does not disappoint either, as leaves turn vivid, golden yellow or faint, pastel red in October. The bark is not as showy as that of the red 'Crimson Queen' but is a smooth gray, pleasant to look upon in the winter.

The green laceleaf is fairly adaptable to different soils, but clay slows them down more than it does the reds. 'Viridis' will do better in a soil with high organic matter and in a moist, well-drained situation. Keep them mulched with pine straw or pine bark mini-nuggets. The green types seem to me less vigorous, but that could be unfounded. Dappled shade is probably more in order for them, as well as careful siting to protect from strong winds and late spring frosts.

'Viridis' has many uses, offering a texture unlike that of any other shrub or tree. In the dappled light of a shade garden, these wonderful small trees are good companions for such shade-tolerant perennials as epimediums, ajuga, or European ginger. Add some wildflowers and mix in some bulbs for a complete garden. Mulched with river pea gravel or associated with stone of any kind, they are striking. They fare well as a container plant and are a favorite subject of bonsai enthusiasts. I have used them in perennial borders to give contrast in height and foliage texture.

Acer palmatum var. *dissectum* 'Viridis'
GREEN LACELEAF
JAPANESE MAPLE

Bottlebrush buckeye
under lacebark elm,
with clouded boxwood
and pachysandra.
Clouding is shaping
the boxwood into
green spheres that
resemble puffy clouds.

My first sight of bottlebrush buckeye was impressive enough: hundreds of spiky blossoms standing a foot above bold foliage. And they were growing in deep woodland shade! A bold, elegant native, *Aesculus parviflora* is hardy in Zones 4–8. Reliable for shade, it will also do well in sun. This shrub needs plenty of room because it approaches small tree status, and is an energetic colonizer. Each plant can cover 180 square feet. Resting on vertical stems, giant palmate leaves fall gracefully from a central origin, creating a large, organic form.

Bottlebrush becomes a spreading shrub of 12' or more, forming mounds that gradually spread out and downward to 15' in width. Multi-stems shape the plant by sprouting straight up from the ground. Leaves develop from ground-level branches, in stratified layers all the way up the shrub. Small plants are the norm when purchased. I have found plants in one- and five-gallon containers. They all look small and scraggly at first, with only a few leaves, but in a few years they become excellent shrubs.

The bottlebrush flower stalks are a marvel in late June and July. Standing 12" high by 4" wide, they soar above the foliage. The inflorescence consists of a cone of multiple, white blossoms, wider at the base than the top, as individual flowers time their opening on the way up the blossom stalk. Long, delicate, pale pink stamens with prominent red anthers protrude far beyond the white blossoms, creating the "bottlebrush" effect: all in all, one of the most beautiful spectacles for midseason and beyond.

Requirements are moist, well-drained soil, with some organic matter. Bottlebrush buckeyes transplant easily from containers of all sizes. They prefer acidic soils but are adaptable to sweeter sites. Performance is best either in sun with moist soil, or in shade under trees or the half-shade of an eastern- or western-facing location. As they slowly become the bold shrubs they can be, space is the only factor one must consider. There are no serious diseases associated with buckeyes, and no maintenance required, assuming the space is adequate. If there is stem dieback, each stem can be pruned, or the entire shrub can be cut to the ground.

One area that could be much improved by bottlebrush buckeye is readily available in many front yards, between two symmetrically balanced trees. In the front half of the yard, between sidewalk and trees, a row of irregularly placed bottlebrush buckeyes would make a large island connecting one tree to the other, as well as creating a privacy barrier from the street. The shady side of the house would be another appropriate location.

Aesculus parviflora
(es'-ku-lus par-vi-flo'-ra)
BOTTLEBRUSH BUCKEYE

Sparkling blossoms of 'Cumulus' serviceberry mixing with 'Autumnalis' cherry, anchored with deutzia and boxwood.
I use *A. arborea* as a specimen; under larger limbed-up trees; clustered in a naturalized planting; in a grove against a backdrop of established conifers; and anywhere a tree is needed for smaller places. Serviceberry is a good tree to plant to be visible from inside the house. Come spring, it is one of the first to show that winter is almost over.

Everyone knows the dogwood. But another native tree, *Amelanchier arborea,* deserves to be as well known. The tree forms that are most prevalent in the nurseries are *Amelanchier x grandiflora* cultivars (x *grandiflora* is a hybrid between *A. arborea* and *A. laevis*). While it lacks the dogwood's showy blossoms, the serviceberry excels in cultural versatility, in fall color, and certainly in diversity of shape and form. It has all-season appeal, with abundant white flowers for the spring, rounded habit, soft green foliage, a tasty berry, and memorable fall color.

In its tree form the serviceberry is supremely elegant. Its multi-stemmed branching habit creates a handsomely rounded crown, and its smooth gray bark becomes a winter attraction. Under cultivation the mature size will be 15 to 25' for both the shrub and tree forms. Add to that a medium growth rate, and you have limitless design possibilities.

This is one of the earliest-blooming trees. The white blossoms, emerging in early April, hang in 4" clusters and do not seem as sensitive to late cold snaps as those of the star magnolia. The pure white flowers are five petaled, an inch in diameter, with a distinctive, pale yellow center. The blossoms usually appear before the leaves, and last about two weeks. The two tree forms most often available are *A. laevis* 'Cumulus' and *A. x grandiflora* 'Robin Hill', the latter with pink buds. Either puts on a good show.

The foliage of all serviceberries can be impressive in the fall if the weather cooperates. 'Cumulus' and 'Autumn Brilliance' have especially dramatic red-orange color. The small, round, blackish-purple fruits are definitely worth trying if you can beat the birds to them as they ripen in June. Michael Dirr writes that they make an excellent pie.

Serviceberry's native range is large; it has proven itself adaptable to either moist or dry situations. It tolerates both acidic and sweet soils, clay and loam, is hardy up to Zone 4, and grows in full sun to partial shade. The photograph shows a 'Cumulus' facing south, growing in clay. A tree of such adaptability has unlimited uses. The tree in the photograph stands by a door that opens onto a piazza, where it is on view from the sitting room and adjacent bedroom, while shading the area from the hot southern sun. Despite the overhanging serviceberry, the boxwood in the foreground receives adequate light, and the deutzia in the left rear has continued to bloom since it was planted. Other companions include hostas, needlepoint ivy, hellebores, and cinnamon fern.

Amelanchier arborea
(am-el-ang'-ke-er ar-bor'e-a)
DOWNY SERVICEBERRY,
SARVIS-TREE, SERVICETREE

The fiery foliage of shrub serviceberry floating above a young American holly, flanked by magnolia and viburnum.

Many nurseries seem confused about the serviceberries. What most of them label 'Autumn Brilliance' is more than likely *Amelanchier canadensis*, a multi-stemmed shrub with upright branches and clusters of white flowers early in the spring. It is easy to care for, with an effective form and wonderful fall color.

Shadblow serviceberry has vertical branches originating from the base of the plant, which spreads by suckering, and reaches a height of about 20', with a rounded crown. An advantage with multiple branches is that the width can easily be controlled to better manage a given space. These trees are fast growing, interesting all season, and hardy to Zone 4 or 5.

Early April finds this serviceberry displaying erect, 3" clusters of the typical elongated white five-petalled flowers with yellow throats. These last only about three weeks, but during their short visit they make a lasting impression. Blossom clusters of *canadensis* are shorter than those of *arborea*, and are held in a more upright position on the stems. Shadblow serviceberry produces the same small blackish-purple fruits that birds appreciate. To best display the abundant array of blossoms, plant against a dark background—a house, a wall, or conifers.

Shadblow's summer foliage is a soft grayish-green, and remains good-looking throughout the season. Autumn foliage can turn from yellow to orange-red as fall brings on a dramatic change to bold, bright color that brightens any garden. The smooth, dark-gray bark complements the foliage.

In a variety of soil types, *A. canadensis* is a vigorous, energetic plant. I have used it often in boggy clay with great success. It comes in handy for partial shade, too. It is tolerant of dry periods, and—given supplemental water—of the intense heat we experience in summer. Transplanting is not difficult, whether you are working with container plants or balled and burlapped specimens. There is not a shrub or tree better suited to the Midwest.

The advantage with the shrub type is that one can choose to leave it with multiple branches or prune it to two or three stems and form it into a tree. As it grows taller, the suckering stems are easily limbed up. Cleaning the lower branches off periodically will encourage a multiple-trunked tree form. At its mature height of 20', if limbed up, it will make a small, round-headed tree suitable for many situations. As a large, multi-stemmed shrub, it can create a natural setting if planted in groups. To show off the early spring blossoms, plant serviceberries in front of, or beside, any blue spruce. Easy, carefree plants, they deserve to be in a prime location.

Amelanchier canadensis
(am-el-ang'-ke-er kan-a-den' sis)
SHADBLOW SERVICEBERRY,
JUNEBERRY

The red leaves of Japanese barberry complement the pink and white of the house. Here we have *B. atropurpurea* with perennial companions of geranium and a white peony. It stands in contrast to a common boxwood, and with Meyer lilac as background.

Colors of burgundy, red, and yellow are the main reason for adding Japanese barberries to the garden—that, and the fact that all of them are so very undemanding. I do not use the plain *B. thunbergii* much because the cultivars are so much better. 'Rose Glow' is one of them. Throughout the season, leaf color is exceptional with this thorny shrub. *B. thunbergii* 'Atropurpurea' is described as deciduous, but it retains its foliage as far north as Zone 6a. Here in Lexington it is evergreen through most winters. Its form is upright up to 6' and broad at 6'. Spiky branches, left unpruned, contribute to a free and loose texture that requires no maintenance. The popular 'Crimson Pygmy', at 2 x 3', and 'Globe', at 3 x 6', are smaller, and have a low, broad form and a globular shape, respectively. 'Bogozam' is 18" high and 3' wide.

Atropurpurea does have decorative yellow flowers in the spring that, I think, look garish if they do not appear with complementary companions such as forsythia or daffodils. I use all the barberries to emphasize the foliage color and texture of other shrubs. *Atropurpurea* varieties offer good burgundy foliage, often with a purple tinge, while 'Rose Glow' has dark burgundy leaves tinted with a blend of pink and white. The latter has a white blossom. 'Crimson Pygmy' has reddish foliage, and 'Bogozam' offers rich, golden leaves with creamy-white flowers, progressing to bright red fruit in the fall.

The *thunbergii* group does best and produces optimum leaf color in full sun. They also tolerate light shade, as well as various pH levels, droughts, urban situations, and a wide range of soil types except wet. There is seldom any insect or disease problem associated with Japanese barberry. The transplanting is easy if one keeps the thorns in mind. I advise using gloves at all times when planting or pruning. Pruning is a prickly subject, but beyond that, no care is required. Pruning a third of the old branches to the ground each year, in the late fall or early spring, encourages new growth.

The reds, roses, and yellows of barberry cultivars are good with the foliage of blue-tinted shrubs and trees. Variety *atropurpurea* and 'Rose Glow' harmonize with red Japanese maples, as the various shades of red blend together. I like reds best with globosa spruce like 'Montgomery' and 'Thume'. The reds and yellows are especially good with conifers, injecting a spiky texture as well as color contrast. One of my favorite uses for 'Crimson Pygmy' is with light brown brick and lamb's-ear.

Berberis thunbergii
var. *atropurpurea*
(ber'-ber-is thun-ber'-je-i)
JAPANESE BARBERRY

Highlighted by a background of serviceberry and a foreground of forsythia, the distinctive bark of river birch is revealed.

Of the river birches, the cultivar 'Heritage' is most hospitable for garden use. My choice of this taller tree may seem inconsistent, but it is justified by its ornamental bark, open nature when mature, and rapid growth. It can also be pruned to be compatible with other plantings in a garden.

'Heritage' is usually grown with a multiple trunk, three being the most common and sought after. Some multiples branch from the ground, while others begin with a short single trunk and then separate. Either form is effective, stretching taller than wide, in an elongated, pyramidal shape that becomes round-headed with maturity, total height between 40 and 70'. Single-trunked specimens can be used effectively in group plantings. *B. n.* 'Little King', at 10-12', is for smaller spaces. A Japanese relative, 'Whitespire' (*B. platyphylla*), has snow-white bark and is slightly smaller.

Leaves are a shiny medium green throughout the season. In the fall, they turn a sickly pale yellow, but do have the courtesy to drop quickly and get out of the way. The main attraction is the bark; it is unrivaled in color and texture, and striking all year. Peeling and curling usually begin when the trunk is 2" in diameter. While there is a wide variation in color, the outer bark is usually light brown or gray, peeling and curling in small and large plates. Underneath the exfoliation are layers of buff and white; the more outer bark is peeled away, the more color is exposed.

River birch is adaptable to various soil types, and has proved vigorous in situations that sometimes become dry. Best performance is in acid soil, with moist, fertile conditions imitating its natural setting—along the banks of ponds or streams. Foliage will sometime be afflicted with chlorosis if the soil is excessively sweet. Most of the soil in my area is on the sweet side, but leaf discoloration is tolerable. When transplanting in clay, set the root ball above ground a third, assuring proper drainage. If no stream or body of water is nearby, watering during a dry period is helpful. The birch borer is not attracted to this birch, and it is hardy up to Zone 4. Pruning is best done in the summer, after the sap is finished running.

A woodsy effect can be created with river birch for viewing from inside the home. A group of several, clumped together, impart a natural, relaxed feeling. Limbing up will display the multiple-branching habit and bark characteristics to the fullest, and perennials, shrubs, or grass can then flourish beneath. 'Heritage' can be a good shade tree close to the patio or deck, limbed up to create a view or left unpruned to afford more privacy. For an area that retains water, is slow to drain, or is subject to flooding, the river birch should definitely be considered.

Betula nigra 'Heritage'
(bet'u-la ni'gra)
RIVER BIRCH

'Pink Delight' butterfly bush anchors the wall with orange daylilies and white 'Casa Blanca' lilies. Russian sage is another companion. Opposite the buddleia shown, not visible in the photograph, several other buddleias consort to create a massed display which serves to anchor taller redbud trees in the background.

There are many *Buddleia davidii* cultivars—far too many to cover in one essay—but the important thing to realize is that you need one. Once you have one, more will follow, because butterfly bushes are not only vigorous but freely reseed themselves. Long floral spikes with multiple blossoms flower freely all summer and on into fall, unequaled for attracting butterflies to the garden. Colors range from white, pink, and purple to reddish-purple and almost black, usually with bright, contrasting eyes.

To give an idea of what is available, I will mention three cultivars. 'Pink Delight' has a habit of about 6' in height and 5' or more in width. 'Black Knight' can become 8–10' tall and 4–6' wide. I have seen 'White Bouquet' 4–6' tall and 4–6' wide. All make graceful, arching shrubs with an overall structure like an open, inverted pyramid, and are hardy from Zones 5–9.

Large trusses of rich pink blossoms, up to 18" long, grace 'Pink Delight' with a light fragrance in July and August. Flowers are abundant on new growth and respond well to deadheading, flowering well beyond August. In the photograph, this shrub with new and spent blossoms shows how large clusters can be. 'Black Knight' has clusters of dark purple blossoms up to 8" long. 'White Bouquet' is also fragrant, having 8–12" blossom trusses of pure white flowers with a yellow throat.

New growth on some buddleias is rich, gray-green, and fuzzy, almost white, turning green as it matures. Leaves can become as long as 10", on opposite branching that lends a symmetrical appearance.

Butterfly bush is vigorous and undemanding. Seeds can germinate in cracks in concrete and between bricks, much as the "tree of heaven" does in inner cities. It does not seem to care where it is planted as long as it is sunny. I have large specimens thriving in clay soil and in fertile loam. Moist and well-drained locations should always be given preference, but do not hesitate to plant one in poor soil. Seedlings and containers of butterfly bush are easily transplanted. Since the growth is rapid and vigorous, there is no need to buy large plants. There may be aphids in the spring and spider mites in the heat of summer, but not to any alarming extent. Cut down to about a foot in early spring to encourage new growth.

Buddleias are best used in a mixed shrub or perennial border for their summer show. Conifers also make an appealing background, especially the intense powdery-blue of the spruce 'Hoopsii'. Buddleias are effective against walls of all kinds, and are unsurpassed in natural groupings with grasses, which lend a complementary vertical structure. One of my favorite associates for buddleia is the rose 'Lilian Austin'.

Buddleia davidii
(bud'-lee-ah day-vid'-e-i)
BUTTERFLY BUSH

A small mound of littleleaf boxwood greets visitors to the Japanese Garden at the Chicago Botanic Garden. Behind it are a berberis, clouded Scotch pine, and weeping willow.

This is a first-choice shrub among cold-hardy boxwoods. For northern regions, *B. microphylla* var. *koreana* and 'Wintergreen' are the best choices. Var. *koreana* does not carry the best green color throughout the winter months, turning a yellowish-brown, but it is dependably hardy up to Zone 4. 'Wintergreen' has been used extensively at the Chicago Botanic Garden in Glencoe, Illinois. It brings compactness and an improved color to the winter garden and is dependable in Zones 5 and 6.

Compact and round, littleleaf boxwood is a slow growing evergreen shrub. Left to grow naturally it will become 3–4' tall and about as wide. Its small leaves give it a delicate texture that is attractive among larger-leaved plants. 'Green Pillow' grows to only 1 x 1½', with good specimens at the Missouri Botanical Garden. With its upright, spreading habit, 'Wintergreen' usually becomes 3 x 4' in the colder zones. A dark green boxwood called 'Green Beauty', usually listed among the *B. microphylla* group, is better described as var. *japonica*. It has distinctly larger, shiny, dark green foliage, attaining a height and width of 6', and is hardy to Zone 6.

Flowers are prevalent in early spring, but inconspicuous. The foliage is the main reason for using littleleaf boxwoods. They conform readily to any shape imaginable and then some. They make fine hedges. They transplant easily from containers or as larger balled and burlapped plants into a variety of soils that drain well. Mulching always helps keep their shallow roots moist and cool, as they prefer. The *B. microphylla* group will thrive in full sun or in light to medium shade, while var. *japonica* does best in full sun. Windy situations should be avoided for all the boxwoods in this group.

Littleleaf boxwood makes excellent hedges for structural definition. In the photo, a tightly pruned form introduces the Japanese Garden at the Chicago Botanic Garden. Using plants from one-gallon containers, or even smaller, is an effective way to create a low hedge of lasting quality. 'Green Pillow' can be seen anchoring a retaining wall in the Boxwood Garden at the Missouri Botanical Garden. Its companions are lamb's-ear as an edging and porcelain vine as a background wall cover. Grouped in threes, boxwoods are bold enough to plant with other shrubs and conifers. A companion of blue spruce can diminish the shortcoming of yellowish foliage in the winter—when combined with blue, the color actually seems pleasing. The foliage lends a fine-textured finishing touch to any walk or path, and to deciduous shrubs. Boxwoods can also serve as punctuation among a bed of perennials, anchoring the beds with form and continuity.

Buxus microphylla
(buk'-sus mi-kro-fil'-ah)
LITTLELEAF BOXWOOD

Young boxwoods of the variety 'Green Velvet' provide structure for this new garden.

Boxwood has long been considered the queen of shrubs for the garden, and the Sheridan Hybrids uphold this reputation. If you have been burned by boxwood in the past you really should try this group of boxwoods. With cold hardiness and lustrous green leaf color, they have inherited the best from their parents. They are especially good for the upper regions of the Midwest. Three different hybrids in this group work for most situations, and are readily available in midwestern nurseries.

The three most familiar boxwoods in this group are 'Green Gem', becoming 2 x 2', 'Green Mountain', the tallest at 5 x 3', and 'Green Velvet', a 4 x 4' beauty. 'Green Gem' slowly forms a perfect sphere. 'Green Mountain' becomes an upright pyramid, growing at a medium rate. 'Green Velvet' is broad and mounding, growing at a medium rate also. All three have bright dark green foliage that retains good color all year. They are all easy to transplant from container or B&B. As a group they like well-drained, even soil moisture and full sun. Part of their character is a tolerance for less light, adaptability, and an undemanding nature. Although I have sometimes seen evidence of psyllid and leaf-miner, it is never as bad as on other boxwoods, and is easily ignored or taken care of holistically by pruning of the affected areas.

Newly planted mounds of 'Green Velvet' are seen in the photograph, spaced to form a future hedge, softening hard edges and emphasizing spaces. As they grow together, the plants will connect to form a low hedge in the rectangle shape defined by the patio and brick walks. Spaced properly, 'Green Velvet' can be used to indicate corners and turns in the garden, anchoring perennial beds and introducing entrances. 'Green Gem' is important for smaller areas where space is limited. 'Green Mountain' is great for accentuating vertical features around a building, filling vertical spaces, and creating barriers such as 5' hedges. Being conical, 'Green Mountain' is ideal for planting beside entrances. All three can be used in descending order for a trilogy of height. All, especially 'Green Mountain', are good for container plantings. All are good interplanted with other evergreens for shape and color relief. Unless a larger shrub is required I use these three boxwoods more than any others.

Buxus var. *koreana* x
Buxus sempervirens
(buk'-us kor-e-an'-a x sem-per-vi'-renz)
SHERIDAN HYBRID
BOXWOOD

The best way to appreciate
the unique blossoms of
Carolina allspice is up close.

Imagine a miniature maroon magnolia blossom, with a scent of fruity spice, and you would be close to the uniqueness of sweetshrub. Native from Virginia to Florida, it deserves to be better known as a great shrub for the shade. I have always thought of *Calycanthus floridus* as a dense-shade plant, worth using for its novelty bloom despite its thinly branched habit. However, given more light and judicious pruning, it will thicken up into a robust shrub.

Captivatingly scraggly when grown in the shade, Carolina allspice becomes bushy in the sun, the additional light creating a broad, rounded shrub with a uniform outline. The scraggly version appears in the accompanying photograph, much as it would look in its native habitat. Growth rate is slow to medium and it is hardy in Zones 5 and 6.

The best part of sweetshrub is its unique reddish-brown blossom with a bouquet of banana and blackberries beginning in late April. The flowers continue through May and into mid-June at least. Thin sepals curling backward and pointed petals that stand erect together create a perfectly balanced flower. The flowers are held individually above the branch by a short green stem, sometimes before the leaves appear. It flowers on the tips of the stems, both on old and new wood. Dirr recommends buying your plant when in bloom because, since they are raised from seed, some smell better than others. The foliage is dark green in the summer months and can turn soft yellow in the fall.

The best possible condition for Carolina allspice is an imitation of its native habitat of deep, moist loam. If this is not available in your garden, compost or leaf mold will do, and if you cannot provide that, then plant it anyway because it is versatile and tolerant. It is usually found in containers, transplants easily, and thrives with very little maintenance. It has a very strong character, and is disease resistant and insect free.

The novelty of Carolina allspice can be best appreciated near a living area. The exotic blossoms and strange seed pods will create more conversation and lasting impressions among guests than the hors d'oeuvres. Carolina allspice is a good companion for perennials, raising the horizon with interest. I like using it in large containers for strategic emphasis where there is no earth to plant. Hiding a downspout coming down a shady wall is a typical situation. It becomes an interesting beacon among conifers, unrecognized until it begins bud formation. However, my favorite way to use *Calycanthus* is in an area of wooded shade.

Calycanthus floridus
(kal-i-kan'-thus flor'-i-dus)
CAROLINA ALLSPICE,
COMMON SWEETSHRUB

Blue blossoms of
caryopteris face down
taller shrubs in the
background.

Its blue flowers and long blooming period make *Caryopteris* x *clandonensis* an exemplary shrub for late summer. During this period, its striking combination of blue blossoms and gray foliage contributes appeal as no other shrub can. Whenever there is an easy way to increase the amount of soothing blue in the garden, one should take advantage. The size and texture of *Caryopteris* make it a choice companion for perennials and other shrubs.

The species forms an low, arching, mound 2–3' tall, of delicate texture. 'Blue Mist' becomes closer to 3 x 3', and 'Longwood Blue' attains a height and spread of 4 x 4'. 'Dark Knight' is also 3 x 3', offering deep, blue-purple flowers, and 'Worcester Gold' has yellow foliage with blue flowers. In the photograph, 'Blue Mist' can be seen at the University of Kentucky Arboretum in Lexington, a calming presence with the hot annuals in the background. I have never seen 'Longwood Blue' in person, but supposedly it has the richest blue-violet flowers of all.

Flower clusters are borne from the leaf axils on upright stems. Individual flowers are made up of longer, distinct filaments that stand above the petals, creating a haze over the entire plant. Since it flowers on new growth, it can be hard-pruned in winter, or if, like me, you are not cold tolerant, in early spring. There is plenty of time for the shrub to recover and still burst forth with a profusion of blossoms in July. Another light pruning can be made mid-July to rid the plant of seed-producing stems, encouraging more blossoms to follow.

Hot, sunny spots with well-drained soil are ideal for blue-mist spirea. Porous soil helps, too. These conditions offer an optimum growing situation that will serve for years to come. The ones under my care never present any problems. Their only supplemental nutrition is a yearly, one-time, spring application of a general purpose fertilizer. They are easily transplanted from containers, and are not a demanding shrub considering the benefits they bring to a garden.

If I had to chose a single shrub to represent the garden in late summer, it would be caryopteris. The grayish-green foliage and violet-blue blossoms go well with other colors, especially yellows like *Chamaecyparis pisifera* 'Aurea Nana', a pyramidal conifer, or the perennial *Rudbeckia hirta*. Other argentines are artemisia, lavender, lamb's-ear, rosemary, sage, and santolina—all prospects for a white garden. A lone caryopteris creates a cool spot within a perennial border, a solution I often utilize when renovating an established garden, freshening the overall appeal and adding color for the heat of summer.

Caryopteris x clandonensis
(kar-i-op'-ter-is klan-do-nen'-sis)
BLUE-MIST SPIREA

Standing over a planting of lavender and a limestone ball, katsuratree connects earth and sky to blue spruces, 'Annabelle' hydrangea, and a hedge of Korean boxwood.

Even though it lacks breathtaking flowers, katsuratree manages to create a spectacle. Reddish-purple buds unfold into spring leaves, cast like bronze hearts. They mature in summer to a soft, bluish-green. Fall brings good color and an unusual spicy fragrance. Older trees develop an interesting shaggy bark that gives winter some texture. *Cercidiphyllum japonicum* is larger than the other trees I have included. I made an exception because of its extraordinary foliage in the spring, summer, and fall. It is the one large tree to have. In a garden, it becomes an elegant focal point.

As a young tree, the overall shape is pyramidal. Older trees retain the pyramidal shape with a distinct roundness to the crown, growing at a medium rate. Total height can reach 40–60'. Width can span 20–30'; be sure there is sufficient space for the mature tree before planting. Many katsuratrees begin with a single trunk and over time develop into multiple-trunk forms, with vertically peeling strips of bark. The flowers emerge before the leaves but are not noticeably ornate. New leaves emerge an intense reddish-copper with purple undertones, and mature into little bluish-green hearts with a matte finish. Fall leaves turn golden-yellow, at best brushed with apricot, and for a finale, release a sweet sugary fragrance just before they drop.

Katsuratree transplants better during dormancy, in winter and early spring. I have planted trees from the container or balled and burlapped with equal facility. The keys to success are watering heavily while they are acclimating, and again during hot, dry summer months. Along with a sunny location, fertile, moist, and well-drained soil is necessary. The photograph shows a tree in alkaline soil with good drainage. It is hardy to Zone 4 which makes it more than safe for Midwest gardens.

The tree in the photograph has been in place about seven years and was approximately six years old when installed. It was chosen for this location because, in addition to its ornamental attributes, it is resistant to anthracnose. Katsuratree is not susceptible to this soil-borne disease—something to keep in mind when replacing trees that have succumbed to it. This is a first-class shade tree with a clean habit for deck, patio, or pool. Its upright characteristic accommodates smaller locations and plantings underneath if limbed up. Lavender, daylilies, and sedum live under the tree seen in the photograph. It is attractive and practical for urban as well as rural areas, for massing in parks, and for commercial situations.

Cercidiphyllum japonicum
(ser-si-di-fil'-um ja-pon'-i-kum)
KATSURATREE

Redbud in a field of
spring beauties.

There is not a better tree than *Cercis canadensis* for spring color. The bark complements the flowers, and the foliage looks good throughout the entire season. I have planted more of this native than any other tree. I recommend it to clients instead of, and for replacing, dogwoods. For those who object to the color of the magenta variety, there is a white one: *alba*. Trouble-free and fast growing, the redbud is ideal.

The outer blossoms are a vibrant magenta color, further intensified with an inner layer of pink petals. As they unfold in April, they are all the more striking because they emerge from old, black wood, an excellent background for the pink blossoms. Spring foliage consists of tiny, heart-shaped bunches of rich reddish purple, right after the flowers have finished. These enlarge into smooth, broad hearts, turning a shiny bluish-green as they do. If autumn weather is just right, the leaves will turn a bright yellow; if not, a greenish-yellow. Either way, the foliage remains clean and unaffected all season.

As a small tree, redbuds range from 20 to 30' at maturity, and spread 25 to 35' wide. This produces a pleasant, horizontal shape with a rounded crown. They do tend to be low-branching, and I think look best when the lower limbs are removed, emphasizing its horizontal habit, while allowing light under the tree.

The courageous redbud adapts to all soil types except continuously wet. It can tolerate light shade, acidic or sweet soil, and is easily transplanted during dormancy in spring or fall, and throughout the season if previously balled and burlapped. The only problem I have had over the years has been with verticillium wilt infecting three white trees. I have never lost any others, and never one with magenta flowers.

Redbuds are one of the showiest natives, small enough to be used in any garden. Their large brown seedpods can be a distraction if it has been a prolific seed-producing year. If this is a problem, redbuds make good background trees, or they can be interplanted among shrubs and perennials. They offer relief and an attraction between flowering times of the other plants. I often use them in front of taller, existing trees to lower the foliage canopy, thus creating a more intimate level for a garden. The redbud also makes a good street tree if the lower branches are pruned up to allow passage underneath. In bigger spaces, I like grouping redbuds in larger numbers to create a natural grove or colony.

Cercis canadensis

(ser'-sis kan-a-den'sis)

EASTERN REDBUD

The unmistakable coral blossoms of flowering quince 'Cameo'. This one is facing south in a side garden where it can be seen when walking through the area but is not in a prominent location where it will distract after the blossoms fade. 'Cameo' supplies much-needed color in this mixed shrub and perennial garden for April.

The older *Chaenomeles speciosa* will be remembered as a large shrub that grew in our grandmothers' yards, with bright scarlet-red blossoms in early spring. They were large, round bushes, with mean, spiny-tipped stems that would stick your hand as you reached for the apple-like fruit. Coarse, dense branching makes quince a one-season shrub, but the flowers are worth it. They come in white, pink, apricot, and shades of orange and red, with the cultivar 'Toyo-Nishiki' having white, pink and red blossoms on the same branch. Buds begin swelling as early as February and open in April in my area. The flowering period is short but spectacular, worth having at least one plant in the garden, especially the popular 'Cameo', with its intense, double blossoms of rich salmon. Almost thornless, producing abundant blossoms, it is one of the most resistant to leaf blight. Foliage appears before blossoms disappear, remaining clean but sparse for the rest of the season. All quince can be forced early by cutting branches in February and March and bringing them into a warm house.

C. *speciosa* is a massive shrub with a rounded outline, becoming as large as 10 x 10'. As a young plant, a dense snarl of branches creates an upright form, but over time, lower branches extend to the ground. 'Cameo' reaches 4 x 5' in an upright habit with dark stems and shiny green leaves. 'Jet Trail' is a white variety, 3 x 3', 'Texas Scarlet' a tomato-red, low, broad spreading cultivar 2 to 3' tall. These three are the most commonly found in nurseries, and there are many more available in catalogs.

Flowering quince is hardy to Zone 4 and adaptable to a wide range of soil types. The photograph shows one growing in dense yellow clay. Exceptional vigor is responsible for its success in undesirable soils. Aphids are prevalent in the spring and leaf blight can defoliate the plant during exceptionally wet springs, but it always bounces back with fresh foliage. Old plants send out runners that become sprouts, easily dug up and transplanted. Most plants are found in containers and sometimes balled and burlapped.

I usually surround quinces with other shrubs that will obscure their tangled presence after they flower. I like to group together a pair plus one evergreen, or else plant a single 'Cameo' with two other shrubs—a conifer of different height, color, and texture and another deciduous shrub such as the Meyer lilac, which flowers later. This Japanese landscaping technique extends the blossoming period beyond what any one shrub can provide, with an evergreen to hold attention in the winter—a textured trinity of interest.

Chaenomeles speciosa cultivars
(ke-nom'e-lez spec-si-o'-sa)
FLOWERING QUINCE

A cascade of yellow Japanese falsecypress 'Aurea Nana' complements the spiral junipers and accents the entrance of this poolside arbor. It is not a shrub for the timid.

One's first impression of yellow *Chamaecyparis pisifera* cultivars is of their vivid color, the second of their fountain-like form. Flat, threadlike, hanging branches create a graceful shrub. With the right companions, this bright conifer is stunning. Its foliage consists of long trailing branches, layering as they mature, creating soft mounds. If yellow is not your favorite color, there are green and blue varieties. There are short and tall, moplike and goldthread forms, all of them fine accent plants that will bring warmth to the garden. *Chamaecyparis* in general have a strong disposition for adversity and are as undemanding as conifers come, but all but the smaller ones listed will outgrow most residential yards. The mopheads 'Aurea Nana' and 'Golden Mop' are popular for smaller spaces.

'Aurea Nana' is a dwarf form of *pisifera,* making a dense, fine-textured, conical mound 3–5 x 4' wide. 'Filifera Aurea' is the tall version of the same plant, weighing in at 15 to 20' tall, spreading 6' or more. The photograph reveals what I originally bought as 'Aurea Nana'. I am beginning to suspect that it is the larger 'Filifera Aurea'. There is a green alter ego, 'Filifera', listed smaller at 6–8', but it can become 25–35' tall with age. The foliage of 'Filifera Aurea' and 'Aurea Nana' is bright yellow with weeping threadlike branches, while 'Filifera' is a bright green color with white line markings underneath. 'Boulevard' has silvery-blue green needles and is taller than wide at 10'.

It will be a long time before any reach their full height, but mature heights should be kept in mind when planning for a location. Ideally, that would be in full sun to partial shade, in moist, well-drained, acid soil. Direct sun also assures healthy lower branches. A catch-22 with 'Filifera Aurea' is that there can be leaf burn in full sun if irrigation or shade is not supplied. They can adapt to alkaline soil, and tolerate clay, as represented in the photographed example. Drought tolerant if given the proper location, they will have better foliage color in our hot summers with irrigation, or a location out of the midday heat. Gilman in *Trees for Urban and Suburban Landscapes* states that pruning the roots will make transplanting easier. They are most undemanding, and hardy throughout Zones 4–8. On occasion there is the possibility of bagworm and tip blight, but removal or a light pruning will remedy these problems.

A harmonizing planting can be made with yellow blooming perennials like coreopsis, daylilies, and rudbeckia. One of my favorite uses for the golden varieties is among other conifers, especially with blue ones, like the globe spruces. The smaller cultivars are excellent hanging over retaining walls and containers.

Chamaecyparis pisifera
(kam-e-sip'-a-ris pi-sif'-er-a)
JAPANESE FALSECYPRESS, SAWARA

The white rain of
fringetree blossoms
among dogwood and
plum trees.

This native has become a favorite because of its delicate flowers and low, spreading character. It can be a large shrub or a small tree, which increases its usefulness. Size will slowly reach 12 to 20', spreading a little wider. Care must be taken when choosing a specimen because its shape can be variable, from shrublike to tree form. I find the upright form more useful if the lower branches are pruned off at ground level to reveal the typical multiple trunk.

Most fringetrees have several trunks, all originating at ground level. They are usually wider than tall, with some individuals more loosely branched and others branched tighter. It is typically hardy to Zone 4.

The light grayish-brown bark is not the main attraction of the fringetree, although it is pleasant enough. Nor is the small, elliptical green foliage, which remains in good condition all season. Incontestibly, the main show is the elegant blossoms. From a distance, the flower clusters appear to be large, fuzzy, white brushes. On closer inspection, one sees the finely cut petals hanging in dense clusters. The flowers are threadlike, with four to five petals, giving a hazy texture to the tree that is memorable in late May to early June.

Fringetrees are best transplanted in the spring, although B&B specimens can be moved in the summer if watered lavishly. In their native habitats they are found along streams and at the edges of swamps, and will do best in moist, acid soils. Part of the fringetree's attraction is its adaptability to different types of soil outside its native range. I have had better results in deeper, fertile soils, but also good success in clay if the root ball is set out of the ground about one-third to assure good drainage, and if it is fertilized twice yearly.

The fringetree can be used along the drive, enhancing a major area, while at the same time not totally screening the house. Hedges can be good companions, or if the tree is limbed up, shade perennials can be planted beneath. Both situations give the appeal of a planting with texture. In groups of three or more, the fringetree will even lend a natural feel to paddock fencing. As a flowering tree for the garden, it will extend the blossom time past the usual spring burst. Placed at the end of a path, as a specimen, it will be a wonderful focal point.

Chionanthus virginicus
(ki-o-nan'thus ver-jin-i-kus)
WHITE FRINGETREE

Summersweet with
white liatris and iris
foliage.

Sweet Pepperbush, another name for *Clethra alnifolia*, embraces both the delectable fragrance and the blossom formation of this summer-blooming shrub. Easy to grow, it is a plant that everyone should have. Color selection is abundant among the varieties, from white to rosy shades, and some come with variegated foliage.

Basic shape is an oval, upright shrub, with dark green, dense foliage. The top is usually rounded. The species becomes 4–8' tall and 4–6' wide under cultivation, but can become taller and wider. 'Creel's Calico', a white-flecked and spotted variety, is about 4'. 'Fern Valley Pink' grows 4–6' tall, and 'Hummingbird', with a tendency to colonize, is 2½ to 3½' tall. 'Ruby Spice' is a darker pink than others, and about 6' tall. Keep in mind that most of these will colonize by suckering, which makes the width purely arbitrary. All are rated hardy from Zones 4 to 9.

Fragrant blossoms appear from July into August and remain as dried pods through winter if left unpruned. *C. alnifolia* has multiple white flowers 2–6" long and forms long, slender candles of upright clusters. The photograph demonstrates this with some plants in the University of Kentucky Arboretum. Flower buds dot the blossom stalk as little globes. 'Creel's Calico' has 6" white, multi-branched blossom clusters. 'Fern Valley Pink' has dark pink buds that fade to a pinkish-white as they grow to 10" long blossom spikes. Opening earlier than the species, 'Hummingbird' blooms thickly, smothering the plant with 6" blossom stalks. 'Ruby Spice' has a darker rose-pink blossom with 4" long clusters. Bees love the flowers and hover about.

C. alnifolia, while celebrated for its fragrant blossoms, is easily grown and demands little maintenance. It likes moist, acidic soil, high in organic matter, either in sun or part shade, as under high-branched trees, or in the shade of a house. If there is a place that stays moist in your garden, try summersweet. The foliage remains a lustrous dark green until fall, when it flavors the landscape by turning a muted cinnamon-yellow.

There is not a more entertaining shrub for the summer. 'Hummingbird' should be the first you try because of its compact nature and abundant flower spikes. The only precaution with 'Hummingbird' is that it spreads underground and eventually colonizes into large groups. But everybody should make room for this one. Lakeside, on an embankment, is an ideal location for any of the listed *Clethra*. They are great massed together under trees, or in a moist, sunny location. They can provide texturous relief among other shrubs and among conifers. Plant one near a shaded entrance, or any entrance that is under automatic irrigation, for a summer treat.

Clethra alnifolia
(kle'-thra al-ni-fo'-li-ah)
SUMMERSWEET

In time, variegated redtwig dogwood 'Elegantissima' becomes an elegant, fountain-like shrub. Here, it spreads over white Siberian iris and white-edged hosta, while providing a backdrop for the African sculpture.

The various dogwoods belong to one of the most important families of ornamental garden plants. I begin with these two species (Zones 2–7) and their cultivars. For design purposes, it is hard to tell them apart (unless counting lenticels), so I will let function dominate. The most important aspect of the tatarian and the redosier is their intense red stems. The tatarian, *C. alba*, has two variegated cultivars that I like to use for foliage contrast and winter interest. The redosier, *C. sericea*, is great for wet shade.

C. alba 'Ivory Halo' ('Bailhalo' from Bailey Nursery), and 'Argenteo-marginata' (labeled 'Elegantissima' in the trade and probably 'Variegata' as Dirr suggests), are both variegated forms popularly called redtwig dogwoods. The former is a shorter version of 'Argenteo-marginata', at 4–5', spreading about as wide, with the latter becoming 6–8' tall and 6' wide. Lower branches of young 'Bailhalo' tend to spread lower, with a finer texture, than the more upright 'Argenteo-marginata'. Mature height of *C. sericea* is between 7 and 9', possibly spreading 10' or more. The popular cultivar 'Baileyi' is a foot or so shorter and wider. Redosier dogwoods have distinctively central, upright stems with lower, horizontal branching, forming a broad, round outline.

On both species, flowers are noticeable but insignificant. Blossoms are small, 1–2" in diameter, in flat-top clusters, appearing in May to June. The foliage on both the *alba* cultivars is attractively long with distinctive white margins and dark green centers. *C. sericea* has leaves that are dark green above and glaucous-gray beneath. Both have memorable red stems that remain striking throughout late fall and winter.

Albas and sericeas are vigorous even in undesirable soil. Good drainage and ample moisture promote healthy growth for these fibrous-rooted shrubs. I have planted them in dense, sticky clay with success. Redosier can tolerate wetter locations. All prosper and show good stem color in sun to light shade. Prune out old wood each winter or in early spring to maintain best stem color.

Redtwigs appear more natural in mass, such as at the edges of ponds or lakes and in parks. 'Argenteo-marginata' is large enough to have an impact as a single plant in a few years. Its variegated foliage can lighten shady areas in the garden, bringing bright contrast where before there was dull space. Its fountainlike form is user-friendly to perennials growing underneath. Other variegated plants, such as hostas, can be used in harmony with the foliage. The shorter 'Bailhalo' is excellent for smaller spaces and for containers of all types. 'Baileyi' is perfect to add interest in the winter garden, like tendrils of flame in snow.

Cornus alba; C. sericea

(kor'-nus al'-bah; ser-e'-se-a)

TATARIAN DOGWOOD;
REDOSIER DOGWOOD

An impressive front entrance
garden features 'Red Cloud'
dogwood blended with
white dogwood and spring
companions of red tulips
and yellow pansies.

One of the showiest flowering trees for the garden, the dogwood is arguably our most impressive native. Some years, driving back to Kentucky from Key West in early March, I am privileged to see the dogwoods begin blooming in northern Florida through southern Georgia. It always comes as a relief to know spring is on its way north. To see them scattered in the woods during their blooming period is one of life's true delights.

The dogwood is interesting all year. Its 4" flowering bracts dominate the garden in the spring, and its foliage displays a good red in the fall. The blocked bark has year-long character, with the gray stems balancing next year's buds during the winter months. The bright berries dominate the show from September through mid-December, if not eaten sooner by the birds.

While the colorful bracts are the predominant characteristic, I also use the dogwood because of its size, horizontal shape, adaptability to different soil types, and tolerance of full sun to partial shade. Proper scale is important in any garden, and the dogwood helps with that by remaining a small tree, spreading more horizontally than vertically (usually from 20' to 30'). As the tree spreads it takes on one of my favorite characteristics of layering.

Dogwoods must have a soil that drains well and plenty of water when they are placed in hot, open areas. Keep them out of the direct sun of a south-facing location, or plan to water them when rain is infrequent. Two common mistakes with dogwoods are placing them in full sun and not watering adequately. Mature trees can handle dry periods for longer than newly planted trees when they reside in the full sun. I tend to plant dogwoods facing east and west, or shaded from the hot southern sun by other trees. As a general rule, the less a tree is stressed for any reason, the more likely it is to avoid insects and diseases such as anthracnose. They are hardy to Zone 5, but if you live in the north it's best to obtain a northern-grown plant.

Dogwoods are versatile. I've used them to interrupt long planted areas of shrubs and perennials, in a grouping to make a grove in larger areas, and standing alone to become a focal point. For me, they bring the natural effects of the woods into the garden. As background structure, holding and defining an area for smaller shrubs and perennials, they are hard to beat because of their branching formation, which allows some perennials enough light to grow well underneath. For an added attraction with all-season interest, try using the dogwood with yellow-variegated foliage called 'First Lady'. Plant it with *Geranium* 'Johnson's Blue' for a striking combination in the spring.

Cornus florida
(kor'nus flor'i-da)
FLOWERING DOGWOOD

Best viewed from above, striking kousa dogwood blossoms float above the foliage like swarming butterfiies.

In my part of the world, the flowering dogwood has been overused. I imagine that that situation will continue until anthracnose becomes more devastating here. However, the disease-free Korean dogwood (Zones 5-8) is a good substitute for it in certain situations. It is more heat tolerant and more adaptable. By using it, you can head off future disappointments.

I first saw a large kousa dogwood in the mid-1980s at Longwood Gardens while visiting the Philadelphia Flower Show. Both the show and Longwood Gardens were spectacular, but the kousa remained in my memory. Although it was too early in the season to be blooming, its broad, horizontal spread was impressive, as was the layering of branches. Before this time, I had only seen younger plants, with a more upright, vaselike appearance. Overall a slow-growing tree, it will attain a height of 20–30'.

One of the most endearing characteristics of the kousa dogwood is its June flowering time. Long after most trees have dropped their blossoms, the kousa comes along to brighten the garden again. The creamy white bracts are separated at the center into four elongated teardrop shapes, broadly round at the base, and stretching to points at the ends. They are lifted off the foliage on stems that rise to float the blossoms facing upward. This means they are better viewed from above. Pale red strawberry-shaped fruits hang from the branches in September and October. 'Stellar Pink', with a dark pink blossom, is one of the better ones.

Kousa dogwood has glossy green foliage, with a more elongated and pointed leaf than *C. florida*. Fall may bring a good blending of yellow and red to the leaves. Adding to winter interest are the horizontal branching and exfoliating bark: as the bark peels away, mottled spots of tan and gray with some dark brown are exposed, leaving one to wonder why this tree is not used more often.

A cultural benefit of using kousa is that it tolerates heat and drought better than other dogwoods. It does need full sun and acidic, well-drained soil, but is more adaptable than *florida*. Add organic matter at planting time to improve the soil and add drainage. Try some pine bark (it is acidic) if no compost is available.

Cornus kousa is worth having in a garden for its later flowering time. With its slow growth, it can be interfaced with shrubs and perennials. Plant near a raised deck or beneath a second-floor window to maximize the impact of its blossoms. Its horizontal character can soften and help balance taller buildings by relating them to the larger landscape.

Cornus kousa
(kor'nus koo'sa)
KOUSA DOGWOOD

Corneliancherry
dogwood is an early
March bloomer.

The corneliancherry is another undervalued member of the dogwood family. I grew fond of these tough plants after pruning them for twenty years. During that time, they remained dense and made an excellent screen between properties. They are as adaptable as they come, and flower early in spring, before most other shrubs. After the flowers fade, large red berries form that are relished by wild birds.

Corneliancherry should not be relegated to hedge use only. With its dense lower branches limbed up it will make a small, broadly rounded tree 20 to 25' tall and 15 to 20' wide. Transplanting is easy, and no attention is required after establishment.

The flowers make an early display in March. They are an exciting sight after a bleak winter. Long before the foliage emerges, tight clusters of vivid yellow blossoms appear close to the branches. The leaves have the typical venation of the dogwood family, but in addition are covered with fine hairs that can irritate the skin. As with most European plants, autumn color is not spectacular. It can be a pale red, but most years the leaves simply fall from the plant still green. The bark can flake off and be interesting with its mottled grays and browns, but unless pruned up will not be a noticeable feature.

Plants can be moved at all ages and in all seasons if balled and burlapped. I usually find them in containers at 3', and B&B up to 14'. Partial shade is tolerated and will lead to a more open crown, which only serves to enhance the looks of this plant. Hardy to Zone 4, the corneliancherry can be used in loam or clay if good drainage is available. Of course, they will perform best in rich soil with full sun.

Cornus mas does make a good screening plant because of its low and dense branching habit. I think the tree form should be used more often, in a prominent place, for its early blossoms. A dark background, such as a brick house or a gray fence, will enhance its appearance. Mixed with other trees and shrubs, the corneliancherry can begin the season with much-needed color. Try combining it with serviceberry, Florida dogwoods, and a tree lilac to extend the display.

Cornus mas
(cor'nus mas)
CORNELIANCHERRY
DOGWOOD

Red clouds of smoketree
against white clouds of
summer fill the June sky.

Without a doubt *Cotinus coggygria* is a sight to behold when blooming. Smoketree derives its name not from its blossoms, but from their hairy stems. The plant is filled with large tufts of fine hair, shaped like pompons, that seemingly float among the branches, so that it resembles a cloud. When it is a purple-leaved variety, the wonderment is intensified.

The common smoketree at 10 to 15' in height makes a tall shrub or short tree. It grows straight up from its base, spreading in a very open form about as wide as it is tall. If not pruned, it can become scraggly looking. Growth rate is medium; even youngish plants can have an impact in the garden. It is hardy through Zone 5.

True blossoms are hardly noticeable, but they do supply the setting for the silky "smoke" that is the real show. The stem clusters that hold the fine hairs are about 6 to 8" long, and the same in width. These large, round clusters fill out like clouds of white mist, usually moving through several colors, smoky pink at their best. Purple-leaf forms have the same characteristic, but flush out with purple-maroon clouds of hair. This attraction can last from June on into September.

The foliage of the common smoketree is bluish-green. Cultivars like 'Royal Purple', with its burgundy foliage, will give an even greater contrast. *C. coggygria* will compete dramatically in the fall with good purple to red and yellow foliage. 'Royal Purple' will not disappoint either, when its purple leaves take on a red tint.

Fibrous roots make for easy transplanting, whether from a container or B&B. It adapts well to various types of soil, including sweet or acidic, dry or rocky. A sunny exposure, combined with well-drained loam, offers peak conditions and thus the best growth.

Common smoketree's many varieties make for versatility. 'Daydream', one of the best, with abundant smoky spheres tinged with pink ends, puts on a good show for the June garden. All smoketrees work well planted with perennials. Purple and red-blooming perennials harmonize with 'Royal Purple'. Whites and blues go well with the bluish-green foliaged types. Either the green or the purple form will create a focal point or be a great accent plant for any garden.

An attractive native American smoketree, *C. obovatus*, is known for its intense yellow, orange, and red fall color. It forms an upright shrub or, better, a 30' tall round-headed tree.

Cotinus coggygria
(ko-ti'nus ko-gig'ri-a)
COMMON SMOKETREE

There is no brighter red in the fall than Washington hawthorn 'Vaughn'.

'Vaughn' (to Zone 4) is a hybrid of the cockspur hawthorn and the Washington hawthorn, worthy of being included for planting in larger spaces, as background definition, and in low-traffic areas. With 2" thorns, it can be dangerous to have around an area which people frequent. Its great assets are prolific blossoms and decorative fruit. As a design element, its shape is most effective.

One of the best features of 'Vaughn' is its horizontal form. Unlike 'Winter King' (see below), it spreads wider than it is tall, reaching approximately 20 x 20'. The ones seen in the photograph were planted as 2" caliper trees, and took about 10 years to reach their 18'.

Showy flowers, coming later than those of 'Winter King'—in early June—make the two good companions for successive bloom. The blossoms of 'Vaughn' are smaller, but overall just as showy, and the same bright white. The fruit matures to a deep red, and if slightly smaller than that of other hawthorns, 'Vaughn' makes up for it with quantity. It holds the fruit well into winter.

The thorns, as mentioned earlier, present a problem only if the tree is planted near a path or living area. The vigorous 'Vaughn' is highly adaptable to different soils and conditions. I usually prune off small lower branches to make transplanting easier, but transplanting is not difficult in any case, even with larger specimens. There can be some rust on the foliage by the time it turns orange-red in fall, but overall it doesn't detract from its beauty or harm the health of the tree.

In small gardens, the best place for 'Vaughn' is in the back, out of the way. In larger gardens, if the lower branches are limbed up to walk under, the tree can be used as a multi-seasonal feature near any distant structure or building. They are great for framing a distant view or concealing an unattractive outbuilding. They can be used as a transitional separation between the more structured view and the natural one beyond it. The trees in the photograph are used to screen a paddock, creating a backdrop for a rose garden in the foreground. If a good defensive tree is needed to protect a boundary, this is the one to use.

Crataegus phaenopyrum
(kra-te'gus fe-no-pi'rum)
WASHINGTON
HAWTHORN 'VAUGHN'

A mature 'Winter King' hawthorn against a backdrop of holly and blue spruce secures a corner of this driveway.

'Winter King' has prolific flowers in the spring, excellent fruit in the fall, and a sycamore-like bark in the winter. A native of the eastern United States, it has a tidy habit and a good round shape, and is an ideal size for small gardens. The selection was made in 1955 in Vincennes, Indiana by Robert Simpson, so it is ideally suited to the Midwest. No wonder this is a tree high on my "best ornamentals" list!

The thorns of the green hawthorn are minimal, and have never been a problem for me. If it is to be used in a high-traffic area, however, the lower branches can be pruned up. As seen in the photograph, the handsome bark is better exposed when the tree is limbed up in any case, and perennials can then flourish beneath. Vigorous under adverse conditions and hardy to Zone 4, this tree will attain 20 to 30' in height, even in clay soil. 'Winter King' has a dense, branching habit, spreading about as wide as it is tall. Giving perfect balance for the well-rounded head is a vase-shaped structure.

Pure white, five-petaled blossoms are the main attraction in the spring, literally covering the tree. They are only about 3/4" in diameter, but make up for their lack of size by coming out in dense 2" clusters, more apparent because the leaves are not yet fully developed. The bright green foliage makes a dark background for the chalk-white petals, with further enhancement coming from abundant yellow and black stamens. In fall, deep red-orange fruits develop, usually lasting well beyond the yellow-orange foliage. Carried through early winter, they are a beautiful sight against a blue sky. After the fruit and foliage are gone, green hawthorn's exfoliating bark, a mottled array of light grays, browns, and orange, provides winter interest.

The 'Winter King' in the photograph was planted ten years ago in compacted clay soil. I have had good success using these trees in adverse conditions as long as they have well-drained soil. The only problem I have ever seen is rust affecting the leaves and fruit, but never enough to distract from its beauty. Plant balled and burlapped throughout the season, adding organic matter to the soil and raising the root ball if planting in clay.

There is no better ornamental tree for prominent places such as outside a window of the house for all-season enjoyment. For larger areas, they are stunning massed together. Grass and perennials will flourish beneath them if the lower branches are removed. If there is only space for one tree, 'Winter King' should be seriously considered.

Crataegus viridis
'Winter King'
(kra-te'gus vir'i-dis)
GREEN HAWTHORN

Slender deutzia sharing space beneath a serviceberry, providing background color for the bed of hostas and hellebores.

Fallen from favor, the plain species *Deutzia gracilis* is more difficult to find than the dwarf cultivar 'Nikko'. The larger species is no longer used because it is only engaging during the spring, instead of entertaining all season. A medium-size shrub, blooming in May, its flowers are attractive for two weeks or more, literally covering the plant in a mass of pure white. To some it is a good shrub of medium texture, with dull-green leaves holding form after blooming. It is versatile, tolerating different locations, and easily maintained.

Deutzia gracilis becomes close to 4 x 4', and possibly 6' tall. It forms a broad mound with slender, arching branches. It is a elegant sight in bloom. It takes readily to pruning and responds favorably by retaining a full body of fresh new growth. 'Nikko' is a shorter plant at 2 x 5', with more pronounced arching sprays of branches.

The blossoms are pure white, five-pointed little bells, hanging from the branches in profusion from early to late May for about two weeks. Blossoms cover the bush shown in the photograph to the left in early May. 'Nikko' has even more abundant white blossoms. Flowering time can be cut short by late frost, but deutzia is lovely when it does flower. A shrub's worth should not be determined by the possibility of its being damaged by late frost. The photograph was taken in the spring of 1999, a good year for deutzia. It shows one under a serviceberry tree facing south, thriving in alkaline clay. Remedial pruning should be done immediately after flowering to keep the plant from becoming scraggly and unkempt looking.

Deutzias are hardy to Zone 4, easy to grow, undemanding, and thrive on neglect, as witnessed by their survival on old properties where there has been no maintenance for years. They flourish in sun or light shade, accepting most soils that drain well, and tolerate different pH levels.

This is a shrub not only good with companions, but I think attractive planted alone and in multiples of three. Its soft green foliage looks good with perennials and other shrubs. Interplanted with other shrubs is perhaps the best solution of all. If it doesn't look its best at any given time, the companions can divert attention. It is good for facing down structures and taller shrubs. Use three together to create a block of hedge as background for perennials like hellebores and hostas, as in the photograph, or a bed of annuals. I like using them with boxwood for foliage contrast. 'Nikko' is short enough to be used as a ground cover for large areas, and makes a good container shrub when planted with other materials to flower later.

Deutzia gracilis
(dut'-si-ah gras'-i'lis)
SLENDER DEUTZIA

Dwarf burning bush
glows on a lake island
in the Japanese Garden,
Chicago Botanic Garden.

Red is the color everyone associates with the aptly named burning bush. Late fall sets it ablaze with fire. It is the most recognizable and most over-used shrub in its zonal range of 4–8. The Midwest is virtually inundated with it. Its popularity is not due to fall color alone; it is also inexpensive and easy to grow. As common as it is, it can be effective if used with restraint. Whether reflecting in the lake at the Japanese Island at the Chicago Botanic Garden or standing in contrast to blue conifers in an urban garden, it makes a remarkable statement in the fall landscape.

E. alatus 'Compactus' is the most readily available cultivar, with 'Rudy Hagg' becoming more popular. 'Hagg' is the smallest at 4 to 5' high and wide, 'Compactus' second tallest, forming a round, 10' shrub, and the species—*E. alatus* itself—possibly spreading 20 x 20' at its grandest. Many nurseries do not carry the species, which I find frustrating because it narrows my options when I need a tall red shrub for certain situations.

Although fall foliage gets all the attention, *E. alatus* has interesting brown and green stems with distinctive corky wings. 'Compactus' and 'Rudy Hagg' do not have such distinction but do share the same flat, dull green summer foliage; they are smaller but with the same pronounced horizontal branching. The species turns a darker red, 'Compactus' cherry-red, and 'Hagg' a stunning combination of red blended with shades of rose. All of these have attractive red berries that droop under the foliage.

It is virtually indestructible. For expediency I have pulled plants out of the ground instead of digging them out and left them lying around for days before replanting them. These plants are thriving today as if they had never been mistreated. I have planted them with success around the Midwest in extreme situations including compacted clay and heavy shade. Their only dislike is continually wet soil. And if water is lacking altogether, leaves will show stress in summer by hanging downward and turning red early.

'Compactus' is commercially used for hedges around parking lots and buildings, unremarkable until they turn red in the fall. The species is best used for large spaces or as tall hedges that are allowed to grow vertically but restricted as to width. Glorious specimens of *E. alatus* can be seen in cemeteries and parks where they have room to reach their mature size. 'Compactus' makes a good hedge if space is adequate or pruning is acceptable, and both it and 'Rudy Hagg' are excellent mixed in with green conifers and shrubs for fall accent or featured attraction. My favorite companions for burning bush are blue conifers and vertical grasses. It only takes a small number for a big impact.

Euonymus alatus
'Compactus'
(u-on'-i-mus ah-la'-tus)
BURNING BUSH,
WINGED EUONYMUS

Yellow fireworks from a young
but well-pruned forsythia against
a background of corneliancherry
dogwood. The long four-petaled
blossoms smother the spiky
branches.

Forsythias are overplanted and abused and a late spring freeze can turn them ugly overnight, but what a show in a good year! When permitted to grow naturally, unpruned, they create graceful fountains, their arching branches bending to the ground. Fortunately, their use as foundation plantings is fading; unfortunately, an even uglier practice is taking its place: forcing it into angular yellow squares of hedging. Forsythia can, however, be spectacular when used alone, as islands in the background, and in collections with other shrubs.

Forsythia x *intermedia* is a large, mounding shrub, 8 to 10' tall and 10 to 12' wide, hardy to Zone 4. Individual leaves are thick, oblong, and pointed, the upper half serrated. The upper side is dark green, the underside lighter green. When not blooming, it is a gracefully arching mass of dark green foliage, unkempt and briarlike in the winter. 'Lynwood', an Irish contribution from 1935 listed as 'Lynwood Gold', has an upright, rounded form approximately 7 x 7'. A specialty nursery in my area, Springhouse Gardens, carries a dwarf about half the size of the species: 'Minigold' is 4 x 5', which should prove valuable for the smaller spaces of contemporary yards. Another small forsythia, 'Broxensis', comes from the *F. viridissima* group, a 12" tall, flat-top form that spreads 3'. The smallest listed that I have encountered is from Heronswood Nursery, a groundcover type at 6" high.

The bright yellow flowers bloom on old wood during March and April. 'Lynwood' remains one of the most reliable with dark yellow flowers. My favorite, 'Spring Glory', carries pale yellow blossoms whose muted color is easier to place among companions in the garden.

Forsythia is extremely adaptable, tolerating variable pH and most soil types. Flowering is best in arable soil with full sun, but it will perform reasonably well in an eastern location. Pruning old wood is recommended after flowering. Cutting back hard will keep the plant smaller and provide the wonderful vertical sprays seen in the photograph. I have never seen any insect or disease seriously bother forsythia.

It is best planted among other large shrubs for optimum effect. It can be stunning seen from a distance. When backed, or paired, with serviceberry 'Autumn Brilliance' and the light trunks of river birch 'Heritage', it can be persuaded to share the scene. In a grouping with appropriate space, as background for spring daffodils and tulips, it is unequaled. Another likely spot for forsythia is hanging over an embankment of a pond or lake. Each spring, I am fortunate to see large plantings bloom at the Lexington Cemetery. The awakening forsythia deserves a pilgrimage there each year.

Forsythia x intermedia
(for-sith'-i-a in-ter-me'de-a)
COMMON FORSYTHIA,
BORDER FORSYTHIA

Dwarf fothergilla with red azaleas and daffodils in the shade of taller trees.

Fothergilla is a glorious ornamental in spring, and becomes a major show-off in the fall. It carries interesting foliage throughout summer and is one of the best native shrubs for the garden. Not as adaptable as some shrubs, it will surpass all expectations if given a small amount of preparation.

The dwarf *Fothergilla gardenii* is an ornamental giant featuring an upright nature, usually 2–3' tall and wide, with a rounded shape (there are recorded sightings of 5–6' tall plants). *F. gardenii* (Zones 5–8) and *F. major* (Zones 4–8) grow slowly with erect multiple stems, seemingly without pattern. The popular 'Mt. Airy', an *F. major* selection by Michael Dirr, is 5–6' tall and rounded like the dwarf. The cultivar 'Blue Mist' is touted by many nurseries, but I have planted too few to know if it is as good as the others.

In April and May, snowy-white stamens create bottlebrushes 1 to 2" long, *F. gardenii* opening before 'Mt. Airy'. The flowers are darling little spikes of white filaments and yellow anthers, usually appearing before the leaves emerge. They have a lemon center that runs the length of the flower stalk and a honey-sweet fragrance. 'Mt. Airy' tends to have larger flowers than the other two, with foliage that is dark blue-green above and white beneath. *F. gardenii* has soft green to bluish-green foliage with an embossed texture, darker above than below. 'Blue Mist' supposedly has the bluest leaves of all. Fall color is best with *gardenii* and 'Mt. Airy'. The former turns an electric orange in October, with shades of yellow-red, while the latter is dominated with bright red with orange and yellow overtones.

Dirr stresses the need for acid soil. I have seen a lot of leaves that had yellow discoloration because soil pH was too high. I have also seen plants here in the University of Kentucky Arboretum, in a lime-based soil, doing well. I suspect the vigor of individual plants can override alkaline soil. When the planting area is properly prepared with an addition of peat and fine pine bark, fothergilla will thrive in lime soil. Give it in addition moist and well-drained soil, and you will be able to admire it for years. After the basic requirements are met, it is undemanding and trouble-free of disease and insects.

Fothergillas are great in the spring perennial border, filling spaces before later perennials come along. At the Missouri Botanical Garden in St Louis, fothergilla is planted at the base of a Chinese redbud with spring tulips. Some others there are under large crabapples, where they receive both sufficient light to flower well and necessary shade in the heat of day. Good companions are other acid-loving shrubs such as azaleas and rhododendrons.

Fothergilla gardenii,
F. major
(foth-er-gil'-uh gar-de'-ne-i)
DWARF FOTHERGILLA;
LARGE FOTHERGILLA

Carolina silverbell, enhanced by a background of redbud. Its unusual blossoms make it worthy of being the featured tree in the garden.

The rare and remarkable Carolina silverbell is as uncommon as it is beautiful, with striking bark, one-of-a-kind blossoms, and probably the most interesting fruit of any cultivated ornamental. This native ranges from West Virginia to mid-Florida, and west to eastern Texas.

Under cultivation, Carolina silverbell usually stays around 30' in height and 20 to 30' wide, but can attain 80' in its native setting. These grow naturally along streams as an understory tree. Clump-forming and single-trunk types are both normal, with the multi-trunked forms having a lower branching habit. Multi-trunks have a round, horizontal crown, while single-trunk types are pyramidal in shape. I have not seen one, but Michael Dirr says pink forms are available.

The blossoms are exquisite white bells, hanging in small clusters from 1" stems. Individual flowers are about $^3/_4$" in diameter with a yellow center. Blossoms are conspicuous, as they appear before foliage emerges against dark, almost black branches, in April to May; the farther north, the later. The unusual hanging seed pods mature between September and October. They are four-winged, olive-green capsules encasing $1^1/_2$" long oval seeds. Slowly these pods turn brown, some clinging on the branches until spring. Vertical rivulets of furrowed black bark run across a gray background when the tree is immature, forming deeper ridges with dark, peeling plates of gray brown and black as it matures.

Carolina silverbell is best placed in a location that mimics its natural habitat; with cool, moist, acidic and well-drained soil. I have used some in clay soil with fair results, slow growth being the only drawback. As an understory tree it is content in either sun or shade. Keep the plant cool and moist with a 2" layer of pea gravel or pine bark nuggets. Leaching from the pine bark will also help with acidity, as will a mixture of pine bark and soil in the planting hole. To assure proper drainage, dig a test hole and fill it with water. If the water drains away in an hour or two there should be no problem. If a tree's leaves are showing symptoms of chlorosis, lower the pH with a twice-yearly application of aluminum sulfate or other acid fertilizer.

Any dark background will show this tree off nicely. Try one in a low-lying area that retains water. Under established trees would be a likely place to find Carolina silverbell. As young trees they can be limbed up to allow perennials to grow underneath. Just remember to leave a branch at eye level so you can lift a blossom to see inside the bell!

Halesia tetraptera
(H. carolina)
(ha-le'zhi-a tet-rap'ter-a)
CAROLINA SILVERBELL

The early March bloom of 'Arnold Promise' witch-hazel creates drama for an entryway.

There are many good cultivars of this hybrid between Japanese witchhazel (*H. japonica*) and Chinese witchhazel (*H. mollis*). With early, fragrant flowers and blazing fall foliage, this group includes some of the best shrubs for the winter garden. Readily available is 'Arnold Promise', named for the Arnold Arboretum. Next most common is 'Diane'. You must go further afield (see Resources) and be patient to acquire some of the other beauties, such as 'Jelena', 'Ruby Glow', and 'Hiltingbury'.

Upright, 15 to 25' in height, an *intermedia* is a sculpted plant that spreads, loosely branched, like a shrub or small tree. Its form usually begins clumping from the base and spreading upward, with branches growing at sharp angles. This diagonal shape energizes an area of the garden.

Except under the sea, there are probably no stranger plant forms than the flowers of the witchhazel. Displayed to advantage on bare branches, they are contorted, almost orchidlike clusters resembling confetti; each flower consists of four colored strips that retract when temperatures drop and extend when it warms up again. They last at least a month, undeterred by cold weather. When the garden has yet to awaken, these strange blossoms appear from January to March. In the case of 'Arnold Promise', they are bright yellow; with other cultivars they range from pale yellow through red.

The light grayish brown bark sets off the flowers nicely. Foliage of some hybrids is dark green, of others bluish-green. Both have distinctively marked veins which make for interesting texture. Autumn foliage can be rich yellow or a brilliant orange-red.

Well-drained, moist soil, rich in organic matter, is necessary for witchhazels to do well. Plants tolerate full sun or partial shade. Optimal growth is discouraged by hot and dry areas. The best flower production is in full sun, but satisfactory bloom will occur in a shadier location. The *intermedia*s readily adapt to high or low pH soils, but will benefit from pine bark mulch. They are hardy from Zone 5 to Zone 8.

Unusual blossoms and manageable size will ensure the continuing popularity of witchhazels. Their angular branching structure, as I said, adds an element of motion, creating an interesting tension vis-à-vis more vertically oriented trees. All of them look good with a companion of blue spruce or against a green background. Lower branches can be pruned up to encourage a sculpted look and allow other plants to grow beneath. I recommend a blanket of spring bulbs, such as snowdrops.

Hamamelis x intermedia
'Arnold Promise'
(ham-a-me'lis x in-ter-me'di-a)
WITCHHAZEL

Yellow blossoms of common witchhazel in October share the scene with fall foliage.

An eastern native we are all familiar with in its liquid form, witchhazel can be soothing in the garden too. This excellent small tree deserves wider use. At the end of the season, when nothing else is blooming, common witchhazel is a fragrant treat. It adapts well to various soils and climates. It is practical as well as interesting for fall, with good fall color.

Branch structure comes from a base clump, twisting upward to form an intriguing pattern. Form has a lot to do with the distinction between shrub and tree, and witchhazel can appear as either: left untouched to resemble a shrub, or limbed up to look more like a tree. It habitually grows as an open plant, which is part of the attraction. Height runs from 15 to 20' and spread from 20 to 25'. It has a Zone-3 hardiness. The overall effect is a beautiful, horizontal, oval-shaped tree with a flat top.

Frost-tolerant, bright yellow flowers have a spicy fragrance that permeates the air on cool days. Its spidery petals, resembling those of other witchhazel species, can survive an October frost by curling into a ball, then uncurling when the temperature warms again. Sometimes they will persist until December. The petals grow out of a cup-shaped brown base arranged in small clumps on smooth gray bark. Autumn also brings a wonderful change in leaf color: rich buttery-yellow foliage can be spectacular and sometimes detract from the blossoms, but together they can make a fine show.

In their native habitat, these witchhazels grow as understory trees standing close to creeks; if given moist soil, they will tolerate sun. Either avoid severely dry situations, or else give supplemental water. Easy to transplant whether container- or field-grown plants, they become larger than the previous witchhazels with a massive structure that requires space. Their size and mass are better shared with other shrubs or trees; it is an excellent small tree to plant under the canopy of established trees. Its horizontal nature will face down taller trees and buildings, creating a natural look. Limb them up so that groundcovers can grow beneath. A dark background will enhance the flowers and foliage.

Hamamelis virginiana
(ham-a-me'lis ver-gin-i-a'na)
COMMON WITCHHAZEL

The two best rose-of-Sharons: 'Diana' (left) and 'Blue Bird'. A French introduction, 'Blue Bird' self-sows freely unless the seed pods are removed; pruning will also encourage more blossoms. 'Diana' is sterile.

Anything that will bloom for three months in the heat of our summers is a gutsy and hardy plant. *Hibiscus syriacus*, or rose-of-Sharon as grandmother called it, not only does that, but fills in a blossom gap during the summer as no other shrub can. In a season dominated by yellow, the color options offered by hibiscus are amazing. Its cup-size blossoms are produced abundantly in partial shade. There are many cultivars but none better than 'Blue Bird' and 'Diana'. Both are hardy and rugged shrubs, versatile and undemanding, lasting for years without much effort.

Hibiscus grows 8–12' high and 6–10' wide with an upright habit, spreading with numerous branches. It sends out new branches frequently, keeping the plant regenerated for future blossoms. If new branches do not occur, pruning of the oldest branches will encourage new growth.

Both 'Diana' and 'Blue Bird' have 4" trumpet-shaped flowers with thick, prominent pistils. The pair represent the best blue and best white rose-of-Sharons available. The former has single, pure white petals and pistil, crinkled at the edge, the flowers remaining open at night. 'Blue Bird' has single, sky-blue to violet-blue petals with a dark, wine-red throat, and a long white pistil. Its flowers close up at night or when it rains. 'Blue Bird' blooms first in July with 'Diana' close behind, thereupon blooming together in a soothing blue and white chorus until September.

The foliage of 'Diana' is dense and dark green with three distinct serrated lobes. 'Blue Bird' has slightly lighter green leaves with deeper lobes, and can become discolored, looking worn after blooming. If the foliage bothers you, prune the entire plant lightly.

I like to use 'Diana' and 'Blue Bird' as screening shrubs, background material, and mixed among other shrubs. The photograph demonstrates how they can be used to face down taller plants and brick walls, while at the same time offering a cool relief in partially shaded areas. The area shown is part of the driveway, facing north, and receives direct light from the east and bright, indirect southern light through the river birch behind them. Ideally, there would be a 3–4' shrub in front of the hibiscus to cover their sparse lower branching. Instead of trying to hide the bare lower branches, I have emphasized it to good effect in the narrow space with ribbon grass. Hiding this deficiency is accomplished much more easily when hibiscus is used in a mixed shrub border with taller companions of spirea, falsecypress, and yews.

Hibiscus syriacus
(hi-bis'-kus si-ri-a'-kus)
ROSE-OF-SHARON,
SHRUB ALTHEA

Looking like a flock of white goslings, the blooms of 'Annabelle' hydrangea with a katsuratree and Siberian iris foliage.

The species, *H. arborescens* (Zones 3–8) with its small blossoms and massive amounts of foliage, is hardly worth growing unless you need a good native for deep shade. The cultivar 'Grandiflora' offers a larger blossom, while tending to retain the lanker, more open growth habit of the species. But 'Annabelle' is something else. 'Annabelle' offers one of the largest flowers possible for the contemporary garden. Because it blooms in midseason in a variety of flowering forms and colors, it is a favorite of many, and deservedly so. It is a tidy plant, remaining upright until rain weighs the huge flowers down. The blooming cycle of 'Annabelle' begins in June and lasts through the winter.

Large globular spheres up to a foot across on stocky plants offer more than enough flower display. For many gardeners it is a lush exhibition; for others a gross spectacle of excess. I must admit to being in the former camp: 'Annabelle' is so useful. Close to 4' tall and 5' wide, it is a good size for even the smallest spaces. Large white orbs up to 12" across are held aloft by single stems. Snuggled between perennials and a background of trees, the photograph (taken at the University of Kentucky Arboretum) shows 'Annabelle' in peak bloom. Blossoms consist of hundreds of smaller florets which softens the overbearing size. They first appear as small, lime orbs that slowly enlarge to pure white, then fade again to light green after peak blossom, and finally turn light brown. The blossoms can be held through winter, or cut off according to taste. I have never pruned them to encourage a second flush of flowers but Dirr suggests he has done so with success.

Transplanting is easy and culture undemanding. 'Annabelle' exemplifies the adaptation of the species to various soil and climatic conditions. With a hardy constitution and pH tolerance, it will grow in a wide selection of soils. It thrives in moist and well-drained soil as well as clay. Partial shade is beneficial during the midwestern summer's intense heat, but it will thrive in sun with adequate moisture. I have never encountered any insect or disease problem with this plant.

With its snow-white blossoms. 'Annabelle' can bring life to the summer garden. It is great for anchoring retaining walls, taller shrubs, and trees. Facing down fences and walls is another of its talents, along with being companionable to perennials. Its big blossoms and foliage contrast well with grasses and iris. In mass, it can be used as a filler in larger spaces. It would also be a superb shrub for large urns and containers.

Hydrangea arborescens
'Annabelle'
(hi-dran'-je-ah ar-bor-res'-enz)
SMOOTH HYDRANGEA

Is anything showier than bigleaf hydrangea nestled against a wall of holly?
I suspect this pink one is a 'Nikko Blue' growing in sweet soil. It has multiple
spheres comprising one huge blossom.

Gardeners in Zone 5 may have some success with these shrubs, but only if the plants are thoroughly protected, and even then flowering is not guaranteed. Although not reliable for the northern half of the Midwest, *Hydrangea macrophylla* is too important to omit from this book. With their huge blossoms in July and August they offer amazing display. Large flower heads come in a vast color range among hundreds of cultivars, from white to pink, purple, and blue, and grow so big their stems can hardly support them. Among the two recognized groups—hortensias and lacecaps—the former typically bear flat-bottomed globes of considerable size, while the latter have flatter blossoms made of large sterile flowers orbiting around centralized smaller flower clusters.

Members of both groups usually grow from 3 to 6' tall and as much as 10' wide. The most commonly available hortensias, 'All Summer Beauty', 'Nikko Blue', and 'Pia', average 4 x 5', 6 x 6', and 2 x 3', respectively. Two lacecaps, 'Lanarth White' and 'Variegata', are both 3' tall and wide.

When it is hottest and no other shrubs are flowering, we can have hortensias with intense blue blossoms (with acidic soil) or brilliant pink balloon-size clusters, or even blue, pink, and purple blooms all at once—a complete bouquet on one bush. Flowers extend from 8 to 12" in diameter in shades of blue to white and pink, all blooming throughout July and August. 'Pia' has dark, reddish-pink blossoms, not unlike rouge, with white centers. Among the lacecaps, 'Mariesii' has soft pink outer blossoms with a bluish-purple center of tiny flowers. All are charming for late summer and can easily be dried for inside exhibit.

Full sun or partial shade in moist and well-drained soil—with an emphasis on moist—are cultural requirements for bigleaf hydrangea. Aphids and lack of water are the only two things that detract from the beauty of bigleaf hydrangea, and they are easily coped with.

Everyone has seen the big blue pompons on display in July and August, crouched next to a house, looking like escaped floral freaks bunched together for safety. They look much nicer (especially the blue ones) placed among other shrubs. Like a noisy dinner guest, their boisterous manner can be tamed by flanking them with guests of equal volubility. A harmonizing blue group would be *Picea pungens* 'Hoopsii' and 'Globosa', along with *Hibiscus* 'Blue Bird' or *Lespedeza thunbergii.* Blue and pink can be rather attractive when combined with pink and white annuals or perennials, such as lavenders, plumbago, roses 'Iceberg' and 'Nearly Wild', or Russian sage, salvias, and sedums.

Hydrangea macrophylla
(hi-dran'-je-ah mak-ro-fil'-ah)
BIGLEAF HYDRANGEA

A standard peegee hydrangea provides height for the supporting boxwood and is user-friendly to perennials underneath—lily-of-the-valley, Siberian iris, veronica, and garlic chives. It shares the space with a climbing rose, a peony, and a boxwood.

I love the standard form of this shrub. Commonly labeled "patio tree" in the trade, it offers so much more than the regular shrub form. It combines height with gracefulness, color with form. It has gigantic pyramidal blossoms at a much-needed time of year, continuing through winter. And fortunately, it is becoming more available, because it is easy to grow and adds charm to the garden.

The patio tree form of 'Grandiflora' usually comes on a coarse-looking 3–5' trunk with spindly branches, looking rather forlorn. Do not be put off. The few heavy blossoms you see weighing down the scraggly branches will turn into a magnificent feature with time and a little effort. The branches can grow at a rate of 3' or more in one season. It takes three or more years for the head to form a well-established presence. In the photograph, the shrub's form can be seen atop a 4' trunk. Open and loose, what looks coarse and ugly in regular shrub form turns gracefully balanced as a standard.

Welcome blossoms in July appear on new growth, at a time when few shrubs are flowering. Individual blossom clusters are made of smaller white flowers forming triangular configurations. Blossoms become noticeable as pale-lime bundles, elongating as they enlarge into 12" long white clusters, with 12" wide bases. As the blossoms age through September, they take on a wonderful pink hue, tinted with rose and purple. At this late stage they fade, turning lime again, until finally becoming brown. The dark cinnamon branches with their dark green leaves are an asset themselves, enhancing the arching sprays of dried blossom that persists through winter. For a later blooming cultivar, try *H. paniculata* 'Tardiva', blooming well into October.

Standard 'Grandiflora' is one of the easiest shrubs for the gardener to incorporate. Full sun and good drainage are the two most important requirements for the peegee hydrangea. It does perform its best in a moist site but will tolerate dryness between waterings. It is hardy to Zone 3 in partial shade as well as full sun. Although it prefers loam and well-drained soil, it is adaptable to disadvantaged soils. I have seen them completely dry out in containers and then recover with only a little leaf burn. The plant in the photograph lives in clay soil. A hard pruning and a feeding in early spring keep it in good shape. It is incomparable as an accent plant. It is also an anchor for the house porch column. It visually greets the owner every time she enters her house as well as connecting the house to the extended garden. By facing down the house, all elements are combined and given continuity.

Hydrangea paniculata
'Grandiflora'
(hi-dran'-je-ah pan-ik-u-la'-tah)
STANDARD PEEGEE
HYDRANGEA

Distinctive foliage and
large flower clusters
make oakleaf hydrangea
a beauty.

Distinctive lobed leaves like those on an oak tree give this hydrangea its name. Oversized foliage and blossoms make it a bold shrub for the landscape. Even when it is not in flower, the large leaves offer a conspicuous and unusual display, creating dramatic texture. I have grown these with success in deeper shade than is usually suggested. Dense shade results in fewer blossoms and a more open bush. Pruning helps, but overall, it is worth the loss of a few flowers to enhance a shady spot in the garden.

Hydrangea quercifolia and the cultivar 'Snow Queen' are two taller types commonly available, along with 'Sikes Dwarf'. *H. quercifolia* becomes 6–8' tall and just as wide, while 'Snow Queen' is usually 6 x 3' and thus can be used in situations where the species could not. In time, both the species and 'Snow Queen' will spread by stoloniferous roots into broad, rounded colonies. I do not have as much experience with 'Sikes Dwarf', but its mature size is recorded as being at least 2 x 4'. If it is half as vigorous as the other two it will prove invaluable in smaller spaces.

The flowers of the oakleaf hydrangea are magnificent in June and July, especially in the half shade so many gardeners find themselves dealing with, where they glow as if illuminated from within. Huge, bright white panicles of rounded lobes, consisting of sterile florets, become 12" tall clusters and with age attain beautiful tints of rose pink before finally turning light brown. The bark is as attractive as the flowers, and so are the leaves, emerging grayish-green with fuzzy dark hairs, then putting on an impressive show with vivid orange, purples, and reds.

When purchased in containers oakleafs are not much to look at, but all they need is some time in the ground to become beautiful shrubs. Container plants are found most of the season, larger B&B specimens in the spring. Both are easy to transplant if handled by the root balls instead of by their brittle branches. If pruning is necessary, prune after flowering.

Oakleafs like a moist, rich, well-drained soil, with a sunny or shady location. Mulching will conserve moisture. Avoid the heat of midday whenever possible. Unless the garden has an automated sprinkler system I do not plant in all-day sun. The direct sun of an eastern location is ideal. Remember that plants bloom better and last longer with some shade. Oakleaf hydrangea performs best in shady areas under limbed-up trees in bright light or morning sun, such as on the east side of a home. Shady locations in the garden can be filled with their bold organic form. In the shadow of any structure or wall is a likely spot too. They make a great background for smaller shade-loving perennials and shrubs.

Hydrangea quercifolia
(hi-dran'-je-a kwer-si-fo'-li-a)
OAKLEAF HYDRANGEA

Foster's holly dominates
this planting, which includes
'Winter King' hawthorn, Sargent
crabs, butterfly bush, spirea, and
blue spruce, throughout the
fall and winter.

This smaller, upright holly makes common landscape practices of the past obsolete. Instead of using gigantic American holly in those tight spots where it has to be pruned three times a year, you can plant Foster's #2 instead. Because of its manageable size, *Ilex x attenuata* is great for the warmer portions of the Midwest, as it is rated Zone-6 hardy. The American holly—*Ilex opaca*—is hardier, but so large it usually overgrows most gardens. 'Foster's #2' is most readily found in nurseries and most reliable.

Gangling when first planted, Foster's #2 grows into a graceful tree with a good pyramidal shape. It stays conical for the first few years until age causes spreading at the bottom. Total height will become 20 to 30', with a hardiness down to about −20 degrees. The dense, dark green foliage is smaller and narrower than American holly, and has sharp spines along the margins. The glossy leaves catch the light and seem to sparkle. As the fruit ripens, the branches bend down under an abundance of dark red berries. The fall combination of green and red is spectacular.

There is no more effective vertical evergreen for the garden. I have had most success transplanting Foster's as a balled and burlapped plant any time of the year. They acclimate better than if installed from a container; pulling them out of the container damages too many roots, and cutting the container can prove impractical. It is happiest in organic loam, but somewhat adaptable to various soil types. The one in the photograph is growing in clay. Good drainage is necessary, with loose, acid soil promoting the best growth. Dry, windy areas are not hospitable, and should be avoided.

Placed close to the house for protection, in an eastern location or facing south, Foster's Holly will anchor any vertical corner or building in the garden. Anywhere in the garden, away from the cold north side and protected from western winds, as an all-season attraction, it will give great pleasure. Try it against a brick wall or a wooden fence, or in front of conifers. I like to use them in cramped spaces or on small properties to add permanent structure, or in linear compositions to screen one property from another. They are good between shrubs and perennials, adding different textures of foliage and height. Planted in a group of three, as in the photo, the hollies anchor the island planting, to enclose the front yard.

Ilex x attenuata
'Fosteri'
(i'leks x ah-ten-u-a'tah)
FOSTER'S HOLLY;
FOSTER'S #2

'Blue Princess' holly with
boxwood in the background
gives year-round structure.
Barberries, blue spruce,
and pines also make fine
companions.

Some of the best evergreen shrubs for the Midwest come from this group. With their dense, blue-green foliage and dark red fruits, Meserve hybrids are adaptable, vigorous, and undemanding, untroubled by disease or insects. This makes them good in both sun and partial shade, and tolerant of different soil types. There are a number of hybrids in this group; here are four that I like best.

'Blue Prince' produces the pollen that enables 'Blue Princess' to have magnificent red berries. Overall appearance is broad and loose. Do not be fooled by the small plants in their nursery containers. They are slow growing, but 'Blue Prince' can grow 12' high and 8' or more in width, while 'Blue Princess' can attain 15 x 10'. Both males and females form a broad, dense square to pyramidal shrub, and can be pruned in many shapes. 'China Boy' and 'China Girl' are compact and round, at 10 x 8' and 10 x 10', respectively. (Female hollies require a male to produce fruit, but it need not be in close proximity.)

The foliage of 'Prince' and 'Princess' is a dark bluish-green, of the Chinas a glossy green. Blossoms are insignificant. The real show is the glossy red berries with the contrasting dark foliage. Fruit production on 'Blue Princess' and 'China Girl' is abundant, according to Ted Potter of Kentucky Wholesale Nursery, with field grown plants of 'China Girl' fruiting slightly more heavily. Potter likes the way all four came through the drought of 1999. Both the Angels and the Chinas produce deep red berry color with large masses clinging to the stems.

All four are hardy for the Midwest, and both survive our hot summers remarkably well. 'China Boy' and 'China Girl', hardy to –20, are probably best for more northern regions and according to Dirr are also more heat tolerant. They do need well-drained soil, but I have planted many in clay. I do not use them in windy areas, or if I do, I apply an antidessicant in the winter months until they are established. Full sun produces denser branching and berries, but hollies will tolerate half-shade.

Meserves are at their best placed with other shrubs for contrast, or against walls and fences to show off their bright red berries. They bring permanent structure to gardens of many different styles. Left unpruned they can, over time, screen unsightly maintenance buildings and undesirable views. Use the foliage and fruit for indoor arrangements and wreaths just as you would American holly.

Ilex x meserveae
(i'-leks me-serv'-i-e)
MESERVE HOLLIES

Winterberry holly blazing
among conifers and lamb's-ear,
with a background of Japanese
maple and grasses.

There are many forms of this colorful native holly with which to indulge oneself. It is an ornamental that brightens the fall and winter garden with stunning red berries. Seeing even one in October, whether planted among other shrubs or standing alone, can be a memorable event. If there is snow, the deciduous hollies will appear even more dramatic, as if they have been draped with little red lights. They are hardy, forming broad, rounded, mature plants, tolerating wet places, and requiring little maintenance.

The species usually grows into a broad, round shape from 6 to 10' in diameter under cultivation. 'Winter Red', one of the best cultivars, can become 9 x 8' with an oval-round shape, while 'Red Sprite' becomes shorter and broader at 3–5' high by 8' wide. Winterberry will grow slowly at first, but over time sends out suckers to form large clumps. *Ilex verticillata* 'Early Male' is used to pollinate 'Red Sprite' and 'Late Male' pollinates 'Winter Red'. The flowers are usually more prolific on the male than the female, but on neither are they significant. It is all about the berries, bright red, $\frac{1}{2}$" in diameter, sometimes persisting into February, bringing gasps of wonderment. The bright red fruits cluster along the upper stem in tight little bunches for maximum display.

In more southerly portions of the Midwest, if there is adequate space, a possumhaw (*Ilex decidua*) such as 'Warren's Red' could be used. Possumhaw is another flamboyant native with dramatic berries, attaining 20 x 25 ft. More tolerant of alkaline soil, it is hardy to Zone 5 or 6. Both winterberries and possumhaws are great shrubs with which to attract and feed birds.

Winterberries prefer moist, acidic soil high in organics, in full to part sun, but will set more fruit with increased light. They are quite at home in situations reflecting their swampy, native habitats. When setting plants in alkaline soil, supplemental peat or fine pine bark is advisable at planting time. Without the proper levels of acidity, deciduous hollies will develop chlorosis—an unattractive yellowing of the foliage.

The species needs plenty of room, but many of the cultivars, especially the dwarf varieties, can be used successfully in smaller gardens. They are dramatic with other shrubs and trees. They are incomparable for winter color viewed from inside, brightening dull winter days. Cold hardiness to Zone 3 makes them ideal even for those without space outside for a garden. Use a pair in containers on a deck or patio.

Ilex verticillata

(i'-leks ver-ti-si-la'-tah)

WINTERBERRY HOLLY

Twisted sentinels of
Chinese juniper frame a
small arbor draped with
rose 'Sally Holmes'.

In my estimation, most junipers are too large, too scraggly, or too excruciatingly dull. Among the few exceptions are the various cultivars of Chinese juniper (Zones 3–9). Two varieties in particular, 'Hetzii Columnaris' and 'Columnaris Glauca', lend themselves to vertical sculpting, providing just the excitement a garden sometimes needs to give it style. Their color makes for interesting relief, while their vertical habit adds texture. My favorite form comes as a spiral. The two in the photo (plain 'Columnaris' rather than 'Columnaris Glauca') were purchased as 4' spirals, and have been trained as spirals for 12 years. The untrained plant ('Hetzii Columnaris') has a tight branching habit that gives it an appealing, uniform structure.

The Chinese juniper is an upright conifer, becoming 10 to 15' in the case of 'Hetzii Columnaris' and up to 24' for 'Columnaris Glauca'. The former is pyramidal in shape, and the latter more narrow. 'Hetzii Columnaris' does have an abundance of pale bluish-green cones, but the real attraction is its dark, lustrous green needles. The color does not change during the winter. Chinese junipers are a good choice for the Midwest, tolerating our heat and our cold winters. A heavy, wet snowfall may break branches. The only other problem I've ever noted with junipers is spider mites. A heavy infestation can cause plants to become disfigured and ugly. Cultural stress (lack of water, etc.) is an invitation to insect infestation. There are sprays for the problem, but frequent monitoring—a vital part of maintaining healthy plants—is the best control.

Toleration of adverse soil can be seen with the junipers in the photograph; they are growing in clay. Optimum growing conditions would be in full sun with moist, well-drained soil. Chinese junipers will tolerate either sweet or acidic pH levels, and are easy to transplant in any form.

To frame a view or to connect the garden to the sky, 'Hetzii Columnaris' and 'Columnaris Glauca' are two of the best upright conifers to use. Their pyramidal form can be flattened against a house or fence, breaking up an otherwise monotonous view or hiding unsightly utility outlets. I like to mix them with other conifers such as Japanese falsecypress 'Aurea Nana', blue spruce, and mugo pine. A background of trees that hold their red berries in the fall, such as 'Red Jade' crabapple or 'Winter King' hawthorn, provides excellent contrast. They are easy to keep pruned to any shape or size for scale, and look good throughout the year.

Juniperus chinensis
(ju'nip'er-us chi-nen'sis)
CHINESE JUNIPER

Japanese kerria blossoms dance on graceful green stems in woodland shade.

Kerria japonica comes from the rose family. A dazzling shrub that is at home in the shade of woodlands, it is great for shady places in the garden too. Stems arch freely, in an open maze of yellow pinwheels. Useful under trees of all kinds, it highlights shady areas in a most refined way.

Broad shrubs forming colonies spring up from multiple stems 4' in height. Briarlike in appearance but without thorns, Japanese kerria surpasses all expectations for the shady garden. Upright and pendulous at maturity, colonies are winter attractive with interlacing green stems. They have a light, delicate appearance no matter how large the colony becomes. In smaller spaces, they can be contained with barriers, or planted in root-confining containers sunk in the ground.

Bright, primrose-yellow blossoms ride the arching stems like so many butterflies. A handsome colony was photographed at the Missouri Botanical Garden in the third week of April. Individual flowers are close to 2" across, narrow at the base, and enlarged at the ends. They open in cup-shaped formation, then spread flat to reveal a center full of yellow stamens. Flowers last for three weeks, with more blooms sporadically appearing throughout the season. 'Picta', less vigorous than the species, has subtle white variegation at the edges of its leaves. 'Pleniflora', with double, golden-yellow globe-shaped flowers, is more upright and not as dense as the species. 'Golden Guinea' is another variety with larger flowers. While the blossom is the major attraction, serrated leaves like elongated hearts retain the delicate feeling all year.

Hardy to Zone 4b, this is a tough plant despite its delicate appearance. It thrives in most soils, in full shade and well-drained soil. Too much nitrogen causes an overproduction of foliage with fewer blossoms. Plant in soil with average fertility, out of hot afternoon sun for longer lasting flowers and improved production.

In urban locations choose a situation for kerria where the underground rhizome can either be contained or permitted to roam without consequences. An excellent place is a narrow strip between driveway and fence, in half light, shaded from southern sun, or in an eastern location. I have used 'Pleniflora', with some success, in a western-facing position screening an air conditioning unit. When available, large wooded areas are ideal. If not, fewer trees grouped together in a backyard will do. This will create a colorful no-maintenance place.

Kerria japonica
(ker'-i-ah ja-pon'-i-kah)
JAPANESE KERRIA;
JAPANESE ROSE

Flushed with yellow
blossoms, goldenrain
tree is a welcome sight
in June and July.

This tree has been on my top-ten ornamentals list for a long time. I use it as often as possible for June color. It has overwhelming blossoms at a time when other trees are spent; and long after the flowers fade, the papery seed pods are an attraction. The foliage is almost fernlike, dense, delicate, and deeply divided.

Goldenrain tree is a fast grower, becoming about 30' tall and slightly wider, with a thick, rounded crown. It is a rough-looking tree until it gets some age, because of sparse branches; but other features more than compensate. It is hardy at least to Zone 5. Spent blossoms carpeting the ground give the tree its name. The blossoms also give the tree its unique place among ornamentals for the garden. Flowering from June to July, the 12" long clusters will blanket the entire plant with brilliant yellow. Individual flowers are small, but produced in such profusion that the effect is stunning. Another favorable characteristic is that young trees only three to four years old begin producing flowers, so they make a show early.

As the blossoms mature they take on the shape of a three-valved, heart-shaped Chinese paper lantern. The seed pods put on quite a show, changing from yellow-green in the summer to pale brown, persisting well into the winter, and sometimes lasting until spring. In spring, foliage appears reddish-purple as it forces itself out of olive-brown stems, turning a bright green as it matures. I have seen frost damage the tender leaves, but the trees always seem to leaf out again, recovering well. Autumn color is not always remarkable, but in a good year the foliage is a golden-yellow.

I have transplanted both small trees and large, balled and burlapped ones with equal success. They have proven themselves in the heat of our climate and through the droughts we periodically suffer. I have placed them on windy knolls with good results, and in a wide variety of soils, most alkaline, some clay. They do require full sun, and prefer to be pruned in winter or very early spring. They also seed themselves profusely, but seedlings are easily removed.

There is no better tree for late yellow blossoms and for cultural tenacity. Goldenrain deserves a prominent placement in the garden for its visual impact. It is a good tree for patio or deck shade. It is the perfect height to hide a dish antenna in rural areas, or to screen any unwanted sight. Goldenrain looks good as a backdrop for blue and white perennials, or with the hotter colors of red and orange. It adds excitement to the fall garden, and brilliant color to the front of the house.

Koelreuteria paniculata
(kol-ru-te'ri-a pan-ik-u-la'ta)
GOLDENRAIN TREE

Bushclover easily steals the September show from its companions, annual blue salvia, clethra, and ornamental grasses.

An unknown jewel for late summer, with brilliant blossoms and delicate foliage, *Lespedeza thunbergii* is a shrub that deserves more attention. I was not familiar with it until I saw one in the University of Kentucky Arboretum. The large, rose-purple mound with elegantly arching branches came as a surprise. I had difficulty believing this sumptuous mound of cascading beauty could be from the legume family.

Long, graceful branches hang to the ground forming a mound 3 to 6' tall and wide. All this growth is accomplished in one season. That is vigorous. The shrub's foliage is made up of glaucous bluish-green, three-part leaves, which give it its delicate character. Knowledgeable nurseries usually carry 'Gibraltar', about the same size as the species.

The beauty of this shrub with its dark pinkish-purple blossoms is immediately recognizable in the photograph, taken in mid-September when not much else was blooming. Blossoms fade to a lighter pink as they mature, and the pea-like flowers rain down the branches in profusion. The pinkish-purple blossoms and the bluish-green foliage create a great fountain of color late in the season.

An easy shrub to grow, *L. thunbergii* prefers full sun, low fertility, and well-drained soil. It will adapt to dry locations and various pH levels and is hardy to Zone 5. Cold winters kill the plant to the ground. This does not matter, because it will grow back. Prune the dead branches completely down in winter or early spring.

Associated with the lespedeza in the photograph are the red plumes of *Calamagrostis* in the background, summersweet to the left, and blue annual salvia in the foreground. Rose 'Sally Holmes' would be a good background too, climbing on a wall behind 'Gibraltar'. *Buddleia* 'White Bouquet', 'Pink Delight', or 'Summer Beauty' would make an excellent companion both for color and texture. Where there is space, bushclover can be used for structural purposes along perennial borders, in front of fences and walls. *Berberis thunbergii* var. *atropurpurea* foliage would harmonize with bushclover blossoms in a mixed planting of shrubs. Multiple plants would make impressive islands of summer color, ringed with *Rosa* 'Iceberg' and lamb's-ear. I envision a roadside planting of *Lespedeza* 'Gibraltar', coloring hillsides, easily maintained with the ever-present mowers of spring. But be careful; once you see one you will have to have one.

Lespedeza thunbergii
(les-pe-de'-za thun-ber'-je-i)
BUSHCLOVER

Saucer magnolia's branches bend low enough to offer a close-up view of its lush blossoms.

In a good year, the saucer magnolia is magnificent in spring, with an abundance of large flowers. It is commonly planted in our area for good reason. Hybrids like 'Lennei' and 'Brozzonii' are captivating. And, for all its lush appearance, *Magnolia x soulangiana* is very adaptable in different types of soil. One is usually enough on a small property; having two would be overpoweringly greedy.

Height and width are approximately the same, ranging from 20 to 30'. The saucer magnolia is a small tree with low branches growing with a multi-trunk. Lower branches are best removed as the tree matures to encourage a more upright, pyramidal shape. Plants purchased at a nursery can be thinned if a tree form is required.

Blossoms are huge, tulip-like affairs, with as many as nine petals, 5–8" in diameter. In the species, they are pure white inside, stained magenta outside. Some hybrids have outer petals blushed pink or dark burgundy. 'Brozzonii' is rich pink at the base, fading to light pink up the petal, and pink into prominent veins. The flowers appear before the leaves in April, and can be caught by a late frost or freeze, but are so magnificent that it is worth the risk. The flower buds are soft and hairy, not unlike pussy willow. Foliage is a medium green and remains in good form throughout the season.

It is not a tree for cramped places, but culture is easy if there is sufficient room for root development. Saucer magnolia will tolerate light shade with fair bloom production. Transplanting can be done anytime during the season if the tree is balled and burlapped. If the plant can be removed from its container without disturbing its fleshy roots, containers will do as well. They like moist soil, preferably on the acid side, and ample organic matter. Mix compost, small pine bark nuggets, and peat moss in the hole at planting time, and keep mulched with pine bark. Do not position the root ball too deeply or the tree will be handicapped, and do not prune after early summer, or next year's buds will be removed.

The saucer magnolia is another beautiful tree that has the potential for being an embarrassment if planted by the front door. The embarrassment can be reduced if the tree is located at a distance from major entries. For the full effect when it does bloom, place in direct view of the entrance but further away. They are grand specimen trees for underplanting with early spring bulbs, Virginia bluebells, and hellebores. Blossoms appear on trees as small as 2', looking like tulips on a stem. It is unsurpassed as background for shrubs and perennials. Hostas, ferns, and other shade-tolerant plants will thrive under their welcome canopy.

Magnolia x soulangiana
(mag-no'li-a su-lan-ge-a'na)
SAUCER MAGNOLIA

Star magnolia after
a light frost.

I have one reservation about this wonderful tree. While it is hardy all the way up to Zone 4, even in Zone-6 Kentucky it becomes a frozen brown mess some years because it blooms so early in spring. It can be highly effective when and if it does flower. But its April blooms may be destroyed by freezing temperatures, so do not expect it to make a spectacular show every year. Still, star magnolia remains an excellent small tree, topping out at 15–20', and spreading 10–15'. Just keep the above-mentioned caution in mind and place it away from a prime visual area (such as in front of the house).

The foliage is kind enough to remain in the background, not opening to obscure the flowers, until after the blossoms are nearly spent. When the leaves do make their appearance, they are dark green above and a softer grayish-green below. The flowers are thin, 4" white pinwheels with a sweet fragrance, not unlike but milder than those of its larger cousin, the southern magnolia (*Magnolia grandiflora*). In Zone 6 flowers begin to open in April, but of course will be later the farther north one gardens. Certainly more graceful than *M. grandiflora,* the star magnolia can usher in spring as no other small tree can.

When planting, avoid placing this tree in a southern exposure; as Michael Dirr cautions, "the buds will tend to open fastest in this location." Since *stellata* can tolerate light shade, that stricture works well. This means an eastern or western location, or—if shaded by another tree during the heat of the day—a southern exposure. It needs moist soil (water during dry spells), and prefers a low pH, but its tolerance is fairly broad, since success with it in the Bluegrass has been good where the soil in general is on the sweet side.

I have mentioned where not to place the star magnolia and why. If your garden has a "room" that is isolated from other areas, by all means use it there as a specimen. If it does not, mix one in with other small blooming trees or large shrubs as a precaution against the springs when the blossoms do freeze. *Stellata* can be charming as the tall overseer for a bed of spring-flowering bulbs, such as early daffodils, Kaufmanniana tulips, and hyacinths.

'Royal Star' is probably the most common cultivar available in the trade, and its popularity is well deserved, with its pink buds and 20–30 white petals (distinguished as tepals botanically). Whether you chose a cultivar or the species, you won't have a better spring-blooming tree—when the weather cooperates.

Magnolia stellata
(mag-no'lee-a ste-la'ta)
STAR MAGNOLIA

Swamp or sweetbay
magnolia with its fragrant
blossoms, growing in
clay soil.

I always liked this native and used it often, but when I learned that one of its common names was swamp magnolia, I liked it even more. "Here," I thought appreciatively, "is a tree for wet places!" *Magnolia virginiana* (Zones 5–9) is a beautifully shaped small tree with sweetly scented blossoms, smooth bark, and a tough disposition.

Under cultivation in gardens I have seen swamp magnolias become 20 to 30' in height with a spread of roughly 15 to 20', but the size will vary depending upon where it grows. Throughout its native range, from Massachusetts to northern Florida, it can be 10 to 20' in the North and 60' in the South. In our region it is a multiple-branched small tree, more shrublike when young. As it becomes older, it makes a large pyramid-shaped tree that is easy to use and to flatten against walls.

Blossoms and foliage are equally ornamental. The leaves have silvery undersides that are exposed by a slight breeze, and shiny green tops. They do not color in the fall, but are semi-evergreen in southern regions and deciduous in northern areas. The thick, creamy blossoms are sparse, but their sweet lemon fragrance permeates the air in June. The flowers open up to 3" in diameter, with as many as 12 spoonlike petals. Late in the fall, there is the added interest of glossy red seeds protruding out of cone pods. When the leaves do come off, the attractive silvery-gray bark is exposed.

Its liking for wet areas sets this tree apart, not only from other magnolias but from most other trees too. It likes acid soil (but will adapt to sweeter soil) and tolerates Midwest heat and humidity. In wet areas with clay soil, I have had good success locating these trees on the north side of a house. The photograph, taken from the street, shows the magnolia's lighter green with companions of Japanese silver grass and iris against a brick wall. These trees offer privacy from street traffic while breaking up the wall. In this location, keeping trees mulched with pine needles will help retain moisture and add acidity.

Swamp magnolias are one of the best native trees for wet, sunny areas. I have used them effectively at the edges of lakes, where there is temporary flooding in the spring. In such locations the lower branches are left on for a more natural appearance, but in other situations the lower limbs can be removed to reveal the smooth, silver structure and allow light under the tree for companion plantings.

Magnolia virginiana

(mag-no'li-a ver-jin-e-a'na)

SWEETBAY MAGNOLIA, SWAMP MAGNOLIA

'Red Jade' crabapple
shows off against
blue sky.

Where do I begin with crabapples? Weak cultivars that are susceptible to suckering, disfiguring foliar diseases, and fireblight have been overplanted in the past. Their flowers and fruit may be beautiful, but there are just too many better ones for the garden: 'Indian Summer', 'Prairifire', and 'Sugar Tyme', to name a few. There are hundreds of other good varieties, depending on your location, so do a little research (carry your Dirr to the nursery) and ask questions about disease resistance and suckering before going gaga about a tree in full bloom.

Sizes generally vary from 8 to 20' or more. The good ones mentioned above are 18, 20, and 18' respectively. Widths run 19, 20, and 15' respectively. Shapes are equally diverse, being broad oval for 'Indian Summer', round for 'Prairifire', and oval upright for 'Sugar Tyme'. A good weeping form is 'Red Jade'. Averaging 12' x 12', it is excellent for smaller places with perennials and small shrubs. Most crabapples are hardy to Zone 4.

Flowers can be single, double, or semidouble, opening with dark rose to pink buds, turning all shades from white to pink to red. Most tend to hang in clusters that smother the tree. 'Sugar Tyme' begins with soft pink buds, opening with five sugar-white blossoms with distinctive pale-yellow stamens. Generally, most flowering crabs bloom in May, and are quite dramatic for three weeks or more. Fruit size and color are as variable as the flowers. 'Indian Summer''s bright red fruit is up to $3/4$" in diameter. 'Prairifire' has dark reddish-purple fruit that is smaller. Some, such as 'Harvest Gold', have yellow fruit that lasts well into December, and are also highly resistant to disease.

Crabapples are tolerant of different soil types including clay, and overall very adaptable. They do appreciate full sun, slightly acid loam, and good drainage. Fireblight tends to occur in hot-summer areas, which means much of the Midwest—all the more reason to know that your cultivar is resistant before planting. Not much pruning is required except for sucker removal at the base of the trees. Keep in mind that pruning should always be done by mid-June, before next year's buds are set.

All but a few crabapples are too large for a small garden. 'Red Jade' and similar pendulous cultivars can add a graceful weeping look, and you can plant shrubs and perennials underneath. Some can be limbed up to be more hospitable to other plants, but most are much too dense. Besides those with interesting architecture, there are some that have attractive berries in the autumn (see Chinese juniper photo). I like them planted away from but in view of living and traffic areas. A group can be breathtaking.

Malus cultivars
(ma'lus)
FLOWERING CRAB

A low-growing Sargent crab with globosa blue spruce. 'Goldmound' spirea is in the background.

This is my favorite crabapple because of its size and horizontal shape. Sargent crab has good disease resistance too, but does sucker freely from its base. It is worth the small pruning effort because it forms an attractive mound and has pretty fruit in the fall, sometimes through the winter, if the birds do not eat them.

It is the smallest crabapple, hardy beyond Zone 5, growing from 6 to 10' with twice the width. There is a cultivar named 'Tina' that stays to 5', but it is not easy to find. Left unpruned, the Sargent crab will spread its dense branches to the ground. Or you can prune up the lower branches to make room for companion perennials, which also emphasizes its horizontal nature.

At blossom time, the Sargent is amazing: a 10' tall by 18' broad mass of white profusion, guaranteed to catch the eye of any visitor. The buds first appear red, then turn white as they open, with the accent of yellow stamens. Fruit is small, 1/4" in diameter, but a delight both to see and to watch the birds devouring. Because *Malus sargentii* is densely branched, it holds a good shape and has good garden structure.

I have planted the Sargent crab in some horrific soils without adding any amendments; I just chopped up the large chunks of soil. They do need good drainage and full sun, like all other crabs, but are just as adaptable if not more so. Their small size gives them an advantage in small garden spaces. As corner trees, out by the sidewalk, they tie the house to the ends of the property. In a garden, they make a perfect accent plant for an island bed, separating one part ("room") of the garden from another. Limbed up and used as an anchor, their size is compatible with larger plantings of perennials and shrubs. A pair flanking a drive entrance, tied together with green shrubs on either side, would work well. I have often thought of using one to three trees, depending on the space, in an island bed in a driveway, surrounded and edged with boxwood.

Malus sargentii
(ma'lus sar-jen'te-i)
SARGENT CRAB

A young sourwood tree showing red fall foliage and distinctive hanging seed clusters. Its companions are doghobble (*Leucothoe fontanesiana*, left), blue holly and Japanese pieris (right); in front is English yew 'Repandens' and yellow chrysanthemum.

Everything about the native sourwood is glamorous. If there is any tree to rival our native dogwood for all-season interest, it is this. From its elegant pyramidal form to its fall color, a more pleasing tree cannot be found. *Oxyendrum arboreum* (Zones 5–9) has an overall hanging effect that is further softened by long clusters of pendulous, delicate flowers.

Maximum height reaches 25–30' with a width of 20'. Hanging branches are filled with bright green, oblong leaves; darker green above and lighter green below. The tall and triangular appearance is rounded at the top. The flowers are fragrant, small, ¼" hanging bells, clustered under the handlike, skeletal stems. Fan shaped with multiple stems, the blossoms come in June and July depending on one's location. Each fan is extended on the tip of a branch, offering the best possible view. The effect is strikingly similar to a flowing white lace cape worn over a shimmering green evening dress of foliage. Blossoms last close to four weeks. Using the same skeletal stem structure, they develop into miniature brown seed capsules standing upright rather than hanging downward. Trees can carry the capsules through winter, adding interest and texture to the garden. Once older, the grayish-brown bark is entertaining in itself, becoming deeply fissured with horizontal furrows creating a tread-like pattern. Fall brings one of the finest possible foliage displays that can range from radiant scarlet to deep purples and reds, sometimes mixed with a rich yellow.

The sourwood tolerates dry soil. It can also tolerate partial shade or full sun (flowering and fall color are best in full sun), in well-drained, acidic soil, and will thrive in neutral soil. But it does not tolerate lime well. It likes to be kept in a moist and rich soil, high in organic matter. To neutralize, acidify, and add organic matter, mix small pine bark with the existing soil at planting time. Keep mulched with pine straw or pine bark to encourage acidity. Other than that, add plenty of water after installation and during dry periods for best results. I have always planted balled and burlapped trees, but understand that container plants do just as well.

Size and all-season interest make sourwood an ideal specimen tree. With a background of conifers to set off the spectacular fall color it is a sight to behold. In smaller yards, a gray fence makes a good background. Sourwoods can be limbed up for smaller areas so that companion plants can grow underneath. They are good to use on the banks of streams, standing alone, reflecting in the water. Unfortunately, they do not inhabit urban areas as well as they do rural ones but surely they are worth trying!

Oxydendrum arboreum
(ok-si-den'drum ar-bor're-um)
SOURWOOD; SORREL TREE

Garden designer Lois Anne
Polan used mockorange with
white dicentra (bleeding heart)
and variegated hostas. She has
wisely emphasized its vertical
characteristics, thus accentuating the brick arch.

Most nurseries carry few if any mockorange, and that is a shame, because they are wonderful shrubs with sweetly fragrant white blossoms in early spring. One must use the word "hybrids" when writing about this old-fashioned shrub because most types used today are not listed in a specific group. Some dismiss mockorange as a "one-season-only" shrub. This is true, yet it is, like forsythia, well worth having when it does bloom.

'Minnesota Snowflake', 'Miniature Snowflake', and 'Natchez' are three readily available cultivars. The first is 6–8' tall and 5–6' wide, rated for Zones 3–8. The second listed is half that size, rated for Zones 4–8. The last one is the largest at 8–10', and safe in Zones 5–8. 'Minnesota Snowflake' has dense, upright branching, with a vase shape. 'Miniature Snowflake' is a sport of the former, compact, with disease-resistant foliage. 'Natchez' is upright, and prone to leaf spot without even moisture and fertile soil. Others can be mail ordered from suppliers like Carroll Gardens in Maryland.

1999 was one of the best blooming years I have ever seen for mockorange in Kentucky. The photograph shows one in full bloom during May, its impressive 2" white blossoms complemented with pale yellow stamens. With its orange-blossom fragrance, this is mockorange at its best, dominating the view. 'Miniature Snowflake' is a prolific bloomer, with double blossoms, dark green foliage, and sweet fragrance. Where space is at a premium, the latter is easier to use.

Mockorange tolerates locations from full sun to light shade. I tend to keep them in full sun for better results. They grow best in moist, well-drained soil, high in organic content. *Philadelphus* are known for their easy care, and for thriving in most soils without major problems. The most that has to be done is removal of old wood every three to five years. If the shrub is neglected too long, the whole plant can be cut to the ground for total rejuvenation. No serious disease or insect problems plague mockorange, making it a very undemanding shrub.

I do not recommend mass plantings of mockorange unless there are large spaces available. Their coarse appearance after blossom time begs for remote locations: in the background, seen from a distance, at the rear of a garden. Or it can be mixed among other shrubs that will refocus attention after the mockorange flowers. If one is to be planted in full view, shorter shrubs planted around its base will help detract from the sparse lower branches as it ages. Another good location is behind a retaining wall of any type so that it is seen from the opposite side.

Philadelphus hybrids

(fil-ah-del'-fus)
MOCKORANGE

'Hoopsii' spruce and 'First Lady' dogwood make a compatible pair, especially with the background of a canary-yellow house. Beware of the overbearing and contrived lighthouse-beacon placement in the front yard. Never to be seen alone, 'Hoopsii' needs other colors, except in the winter when it is most welcome against dreary gray skies.

A few blue spruces make good ornamentals for garden purposes. Some are shrub size, some are more like trees. I am listing three that create different effects. They all have a similar color and are good with other shrubs and perennial companions too. All can be used within the same garden if separated by other plantings. At least, that is how I use them. A friend once noted that the use of blue spruces is a characteristic of my designs, and that is still true. The soft blues are soothing all year around, adding color to an otherwise all-green garden, and are pleasing with hot or cool colors. The most useful ones range from 3 and 4' standards to 8' wide and 25' tall. All are hardy to Zone 3.

'Hoopsii' is the best upright tree form, especially for smaller urban gardens. The others become too large. Growing at a medium rate, 'Hoopsii' reaches an approximate height of 25' and a spread of 10'. This makes for an elongated, densely formed pyramid, easy to place in tight situations. The foliage is everything with this cultivar; its intense, powdery-blue needles put other spruces to shame. Branches are thick and dense overall, and remain so throughout the tree's life, whereas larger spruces open up and become loose and gangly at maturity. The shape of 'Hoopsii' is not always exactly triangular, but it is always handsome and always makes a good accent in a garden setting. By that, I mean that it is best associated with companions that enhance an overall color scheme for a particular part of the garden. 'Hoopsii' is an excellent choice to anchor arbors and other tall structures. It is a good background for a Carolina silverbell, the white blossoms better revealed against its azure branches.

Colorado blue spruces have a tolerance for most any soil. The literature speaks of moist, rich soil, on the acidic side, in full sun; but I have had good success with 'Hoopsii' in deep clay here in the limestone-sweet Bluegrass region. I have had one in clay for 11 years and its growth has not been slowed one iota. The soil does need to drain well and the plant should be in full sun. *Picea pungens* cultivars can better tolerate droughts and are more adaptable than other spruces. They experience no diseases or insect problems worthy of mention.

Another tree form of the Colorado blue spruce with good color is *P. p. glauca* 'Baby Blue Eyes'—not as blue as 'Hoopsii', more of a silver-blue. 'Bizon Blue', a 30' cultivar, is a good choice for the small garden also. I like to combine any of these blue choices with the gray of stone, in the form of house, wall, or rocks placed among the plants.

Used sparingly, globe blue spruce can have a calming effect in the landscape.

The name Globe Blue Spruce encompasses all short, fat, and round blue spruces in the nursery trade. 'Globosa' is usually listed separately from the other short blue spruces like 'Montgomery' and 'Thume'. They range in color from bluish-white to silver-blue. All tend to be wider than tall, making them good choices for additional color in the garden. Height runs from 3–4' or a little more. Regardless of specifics, suffice it to say that any of this group of globe blue spruces is hardy and of good size for gardens in the Midwest.

'Globosa' spreads 3' wide at maturity, forming a round, flat-topped shrub. 'Montgomery' forms a broad cone-shaped shrub, at 10 years' growth about 4' by 6'. The one in the photograph was established in the last decade of the twentieth century. 'Thume' tends to be flatter and slightly broader and can be seen on page 176 of *Perennials for the Lower Midwest*. As with 'Hoopsii', all three of these are used for their unrivaled blue foliage of silver-blue or sky blue. But their greatest asset can also be a great distraction in a garden. They stick out horribly if not used in conjunction with other shrubs and perennials. Then again, there being no rules, sticking out may just be the asset one needs to create a style of one's own. Their size makes them useful because they remain small and reliably consistent.

The globe types I have planted have shown remarkable tolerance for different types of soil. Clay soil, wonderful loam, rocky ridges (all on the sweet side) do not deter naturally good growth. They perform well in dry areas after becoming established but grow best in full sun, in rich, moist soil. I have planted them from containers large and small, as well as larger B&B specimens from the field. Branches are prickly and best handled with gloves and long sleeves at planting time. They can be planted above ground level in clay soils.

All the above spruces can be coupled or combined in threes with other shrubs such as *Spiraea nipponica* 'Snowmound' or *S. japonica* 'Shibori' for blooming companions. The golden spiraeas make good partners, as do such evergreens as boxwood, yew, and mugo pine. When planted in this manner, the two or three should be give ample space (approx. 4.5'), in a triangular pattern, to encourage them to grow together as one. Small trees such as the Sargent crab can be anchored to a group planting and tied to a specific place because the short spruces are the perfect height to face them down, as can be seen in the photograph. I couldn't resist using all the blue I could find with the yellow of the house.

Picea pungens
'Glauca Globosa'
GLOBE BLUE SPRUCE

Standard 'Glauca Globosa' with
the excellent dappled willow
(*Salix integra* 'Hakuro Nishiki').
White companions are a first
choice to go with the blue:
lamb's-ear, candytuft, or annuals
like petunias and verbena.

Standard globe spruces combine flair with texture and color. Dwarf blue spruces, grafted onto a 3–4' tall trunk, are excellent structural plants for year-around appeal. They are useful as colorful ornamental, topiary-type shrubs for immediate height in a number of situations, whether it be with perennials or other shrubs. They work well in containers too. They are also easy to misuse in the garden and hardy to Zone 3.

A distinct advantage with the standard is that the width can easily be kept any size by judicious pruning. Height is predetermined to a certain degree by the height of the graft at the time of purchase. I have seen grafts from 2'–4'. It will become taller as the top graft grows, staying somewhat flat with rounded sides. Overall size will be determined by placement and the space between other plants or structures. For instance, the one illustrated is about 30" tall and was placed beside a dappled willow for color, contrast, and height. Its width will be kept to 24–30". Any more would lead to an aesthetic imbalance and add too much weight to the trunk of the plant to be stable.

The foliage is the same bright powder-blue as the previous blue spruces. The bark on the trunk can flake and peel on older plants but the main attraction of color remains throughout the season. Good drainage is a must for the standard globe spruces although, as with their larger cousins, moist soil is ideal. Pine bark or some kind of mulch will be beneficial to retain moisture, as will plenty of sun to encourage the best growth. I have used globe standards in a variety of soils as long as the drainage has been adequate. Their tolerance of both sweet and acid soils has been an advantage when choosing something blue for a garden. Other than that, a substantial stake (larger than ¼") at planting time will keep the plant stable and standing upright. After about a year the stake can safely be removed.

Standards can be positioned on both sides of a piece of statuary for balance and height. Hedges alone are sometimes enough to add height to a planting, but adding a standard spruce will create another dimension and add color. All standards will provide a instantaneous anchor, both physically and visually. Two flanking any entrance will lead the eye to it while adding color too. Globe standards are good among plantings of short perennials and ground covers. They make excellent plants for urns and box planters for the balcony, deck or patio.

Picea pungens
'Glauca Globosa'
Standard

A young Japanese umbrella pine stands among perennial grasses and other conifers.

The commonly named umbrella or tabletop pine's size and shape are sufficient to recommend it for smaller garden spaces. 'Umbraculifera' is a dwarf form of *Pinus densiflora*, very upright and umbrella-shaped, displaying a colorful bark as it ages. It has a neat, dense structure that creates an older-tree look in a short period of time. Hardy through Zone 3b, it will introduce a Japanese styling to the garden.

'Umbraculifera' is usually described as a 9' tall tree spreading as wide as 15' but, as Dirr cautions, "it can easily reach 20' tall." Even if it does, however, it still remains a small tree, useful for many garden situations. I have seen *P. densiflora* approaching this height in the Japanese Garden, at the Missouri Botanical Garden. The branches have a vertical growth habit, stretching upward into a thick, rounded crown. When purchasing 'Umbraculifera' at the nursery you will see a flat-topped pine with thick needles and multiple branches supported by a short, stout trunk maybe 2' tall, not unlike a standard.

Overall bright green color comes from small tufts of needles vertically situated along the stems and branches. The branches grow upright and spread out wider than tall, forming a short, round, vase-like shape at maturity. As the tree ages, the attractive bark becomes more prominent, curling up and peeling away from the trunk to expose a soft orange-brown color beneath the exfoliating scales.

The umbrella pine's adaptability to different soil types is commendable. Its vigorous growth habit was inherited from its much larger parent. Its tolerance to heat should endear it to midwestern gardeners who want good-looking, all-season structure for the home landscape. As with all pines, good drainage is a must. It prefers a slightly acidic soil, but will thrive in many different types. Pine bark mulch dug into the hole at planting time will help. Full sun is necessary to ensure characteristically dense growth.

No other pine better represents the simplicity of the Japanese style. A single tree seen across a pool can evoke the calm feeling of a peaceful place. This pine has an affinity for stone. With its upright branching habit there is space and light for plants to flourish beneath. Providing structural support for the garden is easy with a pine that fits into small spaces. 'Umbraculifera' is an excellent choice for large planters on a patio or deck when kept pruned to stay smaller. Given center stage as a featured tree, it will lend interest all year.

Pinus densiflora
'Umbraculifera'
(pi'-nus den-si-flo'-ra)
UMBRELLA PINE,
JAPANESE RED PINE

The traditional Japanese way to use mugo pine—with sculpted azaleas.
The low, mounded evergreen forms of mugo are easily used in the garden
or landscape. They are excellent for connecting larger evergreens, or any
taller plants, together.

Hearing the phrase "Japanese garden," what gardener does not think of a mugo pine with swirling white sand raked around it: an island in a body of water? But after a few years, as many have learned to their sorrow, some forms of *Pinus mugo* may no longer be a neat and tidy green mound. Unless properly spaced or regularly pruned, they may overgrow a sidewalk or outgrow a foundation planting. Mugo pine can make an excellent addition to our gardens and landscapes, holding and anchoring many different planting combinations, if its mature size is kept in mind.

While the species can become as tall as 75', the mugos of concern to gardeners are those carried by nurseries, labeled something like "Mugo Dwarf," which are low, slow-growing, broad-spreading shrubs that will remain under 10'. There are some recognized cultivars—'Compacta', 'Gnom', 'Mops', and var. *pumilio*, to name a few—but if no cultivar name is given, be prepared to prune during the lifetime of the plant unless you have been extremely generous about spacing. 'Compacta' is a good round form; old plants (30–40 years) can be 4 x 4' to 5' (other listings have it at 3'). One source lists 'Gnom' as 15 x 36", while another has 'Gnome' at 12'. Take precautions against confusion by knowing what is being sold. All are hardy through Zone 3.

Needles are displayed horizontally all around the stems, giving the branches an appealing bottlebrush look. In the best cultivars, tight clusters of dark green needles face upward to create a smooth, rounded form. Mugo usually stays low and small. The annual growth rate varies from 1" with 'Mitsch Mini' to 3 to 5" a year with faster-growing cultivars. It blends well into a mixed planting of perennials and/or other conifers. 'Aurea' and 'Ophir' have yellow needles in the winter.

Most mugo pines purchased at local nurseries will be in containers. Larger ones can be found B&B. Either will transplant and adapt readily to deep loam in full sun. These are ideal growing conditions, but mugos will also tolerate partial shade as well as a sweeter, less hospitable soil. If in clay, they will benefit from pine bark mixed in the hole at planting time and from being set above ground level for better drainage.

As a low, green transition among perennials and shrubs, mugos create permanent structure and contrast. Good shrub companions are *Syringa meyeri* 'Palibin' and *Taxus* 'Densiformis'. Planting these three together in any configuration will make an interesting combination of color and texture. Boxwood and stone with mugo creates a Japanese touch. Because mugos grow slowly, they make good container plants.

Pinus mugo
(pi'-nus mu'-go)
MUGO PINE

The low growing version of
dwarf eastern white pine
'Nana' in an island planting
with azaleas, crabapple, and
yew. If a small planting is
too flat, some interest can be
injected by using the taller-
type 'Nana' as a standard.

Of all the native white pines available for ornamental use in the garden, *Pinus strobus* 'Nana' is one of the best. Unlike its tall parent, this qualifies as a dwarf, the only white pine in the shape of a low-growing mound. When space is limited, you will be much better off choosing from the different forms of 'Nana' rather than using the conventional white pine.

While variations of 'Nana' can be anything from low-growing mounds to 15–20' trees, nurseries normally offer mound forms at 1–3'. Regardless of mature size, all grow at a slow to very slow rate and are hardy in Zones 3–8. One of my favorites for its immediate shape and height is a standard type with a graft 3–4' above the trunk. With its higher branches, annuals, ground covers, and perennials can thrive underneath. In the grafted form, the head is usually about 3' across. Its diameter can be maintained at 3' or permitted to become wider and taller. Some other cultivars are 'Compacta', 'Blue Shag', and 'Sea Urchin'. 'Blue Shag' in 15 years can become 4 x 5' to 5 x 6'. 'Sea Urchin' qualifies as a miniature suitable for trough planting, growing 2 to 3' in about 10 years.

'Nana' has soft, silvery-green needles that take on a bluish tint in the proper light. The upper side of the needle carries the green color, while the underside is tinted with silver-white, lending a fine texture to the overall appearance, and complementing any color scheme. New spring growth is lime-green, in the characteristic form of "candles."

White pines prefer full sun but will tolerate light shade. Good drainage and fertile soil are necessary if they are to grow their best. Tall white pines are susceptible to strong winds, but the shorter 'Nana' has no such problem. They are said to be intolerant of air pollutants, although often used in urban locations, and also to salt. However, for the Midwest, they seem to thrive in most situations, surviving in dry, rocky soil and in wet and humid places. In sweeter soils, *Pinus strobus* and cultivars will develop chlorosis. I have used them with success in clay soils that drain well.

Structure is one of the major characteristics that define a garden, integrating all the plantings and features. 'Nana' standards are excellent for creating a formal appearance or lending an immediate Japanese-style topiary effect. I usually permit the head of the standard type 'Nana' to spread horizontally more than vertically. Such a shape helps anchor a planting to other parts of the garden. Placing the low-mounding types with stones and with other shrubs of similar shape is effective. Either type is unbeatable for producing all-season structure in the garden.

Pinus strobus
'Nana' (standard)
(pi'-nus stro'-bus)
DWARF EASTERN
WHITE PINE

Facing down a wall in
April is cherry laurel
'Otto Luyken'.

The beauty of these two cherrylaurels is due not only to their prolific spring flowers and lustrous green foliage, but to the fact that they maintain this foliage throughout most winters, even in the shade. 'Otto Luyken' (rated as hardy to Zone 6) and 'Schipkaensis' (Zone 5) both develop into fine, spreading shrubs that remain dark green and offer one of the best resources for shady situations. Comparable in price to boxwood but very different in texture, cherrylaurel usually does better than boxwood in deeper shade. We are fortunate to have it, because there is always shade to contend with.

While the species can grow up to 20' it is the more manageable cultivars that are readily available. 'Otto Luyken' spreads 3' x 4'. The 4" long, narrow leaves congregate on the branches at an angle to the stems for an upward, flowing movement, giving it a distinction not shared by 'Schipkaensis'. Shiny, abundant green leaves give both cultivars a rich presence in the garden, not unlike that of our native mountain laurel. 'Otto Luyken', seen in this April photograph, is close to its mature size, anchoring a wall as well as connecting perennials with trees. The larger 'Schipkaensis' becomes 4' x 5–10' and is the choice for Zone 5 residents.

From April to May, dense white spikes of blossoms stand erect on 5" long stems, covering the entire plant and really brightening shady places. Pure white petals spread out beneath a center cluster of erect stamens to form each blossom. The blossoms mature into clusters of small, cherry-like fruit, first red, later turning black. They are not palatable to humans, but soon disappear.

Cherrylaurels are usually found in containers, but larger B&B specimens are sometimes available. They transplant easily, and will thrive in full sun or shade given moist, well-drained, highly organic soil. Use some peat moss or pine bark mini-nuggets in the hole at planting time to insure a good start for it. To reshape or renew a cherrylaurel, prune in spring or late summer.

Taking into account future as well as present conditions, Cherrylaurels are an excellent choice to make the transition from sun to shade. They are good for planting in mass to create a hedge or a green backdrop for perennials and annuals, as well as planting under trees. They are good with shady compatriots like yews and boxwood.

Prunus laurocerasus
(pru'-nus lar-o-ser-a'-sus)
COMMON CHERRYLAUREL, ENGLISH LAUREL

The lush pink blossoms of dwarf ornamental peach. Peaches do require some work to keep them in shape, but the effort is rewarding. A judicious pruning back every couple of years will keep them looking and flowering their best and encourage more fruit. The flowering specimen in the photograph is eleven years old and has attained a height of 5'. When purchased, this was simply labeled "dwarf peach."

Blooming along with Bradford pears and flowering plums, a more beautiful presence cannot be found in early April than the dwarf varieties of *Prunus persica*. There are many cultivars of the peach, but I will discuss a few that are valuable as ornamentals.

Pink 'Bonanza' is the most common peach sold as a dwarf; 'Early Doubles' cultivars come in 'Pink', 'Red', and 'White'. There is also a 'Dwarf Mandarin Peach' available in the Midwest. Most maintain a rounded crown, branching upward with dark green leaves. The ultimate shape turns out to be short and broad, up to 15'.

The main show with dwarf peaches is their bright, vivid blossoms in early April. Blossom time puts them in danger from late frosts, but the possibility of those brilliant blossoms makes the risk worth taking. Flower colors range from white to red, striped, and multicolored. They come in single, semi-double, and double-flowering forms. The plant in the photograph first comes out as a dark pink, fading to a lighter pink, while maintaining a darker pink throat. In some years the foliage will provide a deep yellow fall display, but do not count on it.

The best situation for the dwarf peach is a location in full sun, with well-drained moist, acidic soil. There is some tolerance to less than ideal soil. The one shown in the photograph was planted in clay soil that drains well but had been compacted by the neighbor's house construction. It is often said that peaches should be avoided because of multiple problems with aphids, borers, and various stem diseases. Despite these warnings, I remain confident that they are worthy of use because of the blossoms. Usually found in containers, *Prunus persica* is best planted in the spring.

I would not place the dwarf peach in a prominent area because it has a rough appearance when not in flower. To use its form to advantage, and to keep its shape visually uncluttered, I recommend planting this small tree where it can stand alone and be viewed from a distance, or where low-growing perennials or annuals can be placed underneath as a distraction. It is good to use at the end of a row of taller trees or shrubs as an element to decrease the height and flatness created by the taller companions. Their blossom is a good way to attract attention to an area of the garden in the spring. Located outside a favorite window, it creates a beautiful spring view. Underplanting with snowdrops or crocus would further increase the spring treat. Try a dwarf peach; I think you will see for yourself that it is worth the effort.

Prunus persica
(pru'-nus per'si-ca)
DWARF ORNAMENTAL
PEACH

'Kwanzan' used as the taller element with leatherleaf viburnum in this tall hedge that screens a building from street traffic.

132

Both of these early blooming cherries are magnificent, each in its own way. Both have an attractive double blossom and early fall color and are fast growers. Because the more popular 'Kwanzan' ('Sekiyama') needs no promotion, I'll emphasize 'Shogetsu', which should be used more. Ask your nursery to order it if they do not carry it. The 1½" caliper (10–12') size is carried by Landscape Supply in northern Kentucky (see Resources).

Between 15 and 18', 'Shogetsu's smaller size and round-upright branch formation make it a better choice for smaller properties than 'Kwanzan', which can attain a stature of 30 to 40' when grown on its own roots (not grafted). However, the specimens of 'Shogetsu' I have planted have all been grafted, the branches spreading upward from a single, straight trunk to form a broad, flattened crown, almost the perfect "Y" shape. The non-grafted types form a low, broad head.

The flowers on both cultivars hang in long clusters along the branches well before the foliage comes out to obscure their beauty. 'Kwanzan' has 2½" dark pink flowers, while 'Shogetsu' has 2" lighter pink flowers that quickly fade to white, with dainty, frilled outer edges. Both bloom abundantly. Dark bark, typically reddish-brown, etched with horizontal lenticels, provides an excellent background for blossom display. At maturity 'Shogetsu' is clothed in dark green leaves, creased by a distinct midrib, with veins running straight out to the slightly serrated leaf edges. 'Kwanzan' has the distinction of having the best fall color in the genus.

As with most cherries, full sun is necessary for good health. They will tolerate some clay if well-drained, but prefer a better soil. I've transplanted 'Shogetsu' balled and burlapped and 'Kwanzan' from containers with success. All acclimated without the slightest difficulty. There is no fruit production, but in a good fall the foliage of 'Shogetsu' turns a smooth butter-yellow. 'Kwanzan' goes it one better by turning a memorable bronzey-orange. Their lifespan can be limited by borers, cankers, and virus, but even so, you can expect them to give pleasure for 15 to 25 years, which is more than enough.

'Shogetsu' maintains a structural uniformity like that of 'Kwanzan', making it a perfect tree to complement a building, drive entrance, or doorway. In the garden, I have used 'Shogetsu' to create an allée on the back side of a formal rose garden, with hawthorn on the opposite side. This would also make a striking combination planted in conjunction with 'Kwanzan' and Yoshino cherry.

Prunus serrulata
'Kwanzan', 'Shogetsu'
(pru'-nus ser-u-la'-ta)
JAPANESE CHERRY

The blessing of 'Autumnalis'
cherry, seen in mid-March. This
specimen has a single trunk of 4'
before it branches. Branches are
not so dense as to discourage
underplantings; necessary light
for shade-loving perennials and
shrubs can penetrate. 'Autumnalis'
looks good underplanted with
perennials such as hostas, epimedium, or Virginia bluebells.

This little tree is so named because it flowers in the fall as well as in the spring. While the fall blooms are not so abundant, they are still a rare treat. *Prunus subhirtella* 'Autumnalis' also remains small, neat in branch formation, and relatively carefree. When I need a small pink-flowering tree for a garden, 'Autumnalis' is what I use.

Autumn cherry becomes a well-groomed, oval-shaped tree. It characteristically grows from a single trunk that forks low to the ground. 'Autumnalis' is fast growing and usually attains 20' under cultivation, reaching a possible 40'. Unlike other cherries, the *subhirtella* group tends to be long-lived and disease resistant.

Semi-double, light pink petals are rich and plentiful in early to late March, usually flowering along with the serviceberries. The buds are a darker pink when they emerge, fading to a lighter pink when opening, then white as they mature. Dark branches make an excellent background as small flower clusters cover the tree. After the spring flower show, the foliage emerges a dark green with the typical serrated edges. If the fall is warm, pink blossoms will again appear.

The 'Autumnalis' in the photograph is in clay soil that drains well, which slows its growth. Still, situated in this sunny position, it has served this garden for eleven years, attaining a height of about 18'. Other than pruning inside dead branches and removing a branch that was hanging into the adjacent path, maintenance has been minimal. It has been fertilized every other year with tree spikes, and receives some residual fertilizer when the lawn and beds around it are fed. As with all trees when first planted, you should water often enough to keep the root ball moist. When established they are stress tolerant, but watering is advised when there has been no rain for a month.

'Autumnalis' is a reliable tree for small places, where the garden cries out for immediate structure and early spring color. As a focal point when blooming, 'Autumnalis' will direct attention anywhere it is placed: to the end of a pathway, showing above a wall to divert one's eye in a certain direction, or standing with and above shrubs to anchor any given spot. Spring blossoms are best displayed against a solid background, such as conifers (especially blue ones) or a building. They are highly effective near water where their reflection increases the pink drama of spring blossom. Difficult to use incorrectly, a better choice couldn't be found for a small tree near the house, or in the garden.

Prunus subhirtella
'Autumnalis'
(pru'nus sub-her-tel'luh)
AUTUMN CHERRY

The graceful weeping
cherry 'Pendula' is
always breathtaking.
Standing under one
in full flower is like
being under a pink
waterfall.

The Higan cherry (*Higan* means spring equinox, according to *Japanese Flowering Cherries* by Wybe Kuitert) has been a favorite since I first began designing gardens. One of the best flowering cherries for stressful conditions, it tolerates temperature extremes. With its graceful branches covered with blossoms, arching to the ground, there is not a more dramatic flowering tree.

Commonly called weeping cherries, Higans are fast-growing. Flowering as young trees, they can make a bold statement in 5 years, reaching 20–30' in height and 20–25' in width. The example in the photograph is ten years old and 20' x 16'. A vertical emphasis is balanced with the horizontal spread of pendulous branches, structurally handsome in winter and colorful in spring. Hardy to Zone 5, the Higan is usually found grafted on 6 feet of understock in seven-gallon containers or B&B up to 3" caliper.

From March to April, single pink blossoms hang from the arching branches in clusters of 2 to 5. The pink flowers cover the bare branches, first as dark pink buds, then opening to candy-pink as seen in the photograph, and finally fading to white. The tree's graceful structure is created by major branches lifting vertically from the graft, allowing the secondary branches to cascade downward. Dark, reddish-brown bark is brushed with a top layer of silver, typically striped with horizontal air ports (lenticels). Such plants as boxwood and ivy will grow satisfactorily beneath its branches.

Growth rate is rapid, even in the worst soils. The tree in the photograph is growing in sticky, yellow clay. As with other cherries, 'Pendula' requires full sun and well-drained soil. Beyond that they are very adaptable and long-lived. Regardless of soil type, I fertilize yearly with a nutritionally balanced tree spike. Otherwise, removing dead and unwanted branches and giving supplemental water during acclimation is all that is necessary.

The Higan in the photograph is one of two on either side of a stairway leading to a lower garden room. From the pool area, their placement was made to frame the stairway, to create a living arch to walk under and to screen out wires and houses at the back of the property. Being placed closer to the living area, they perform this chore better than the trees along the back boundary. This has created privacy in a short time, as viewed from the rear exit of the house and the pool area. This is a good tree for many locations as long as it is given room to spread.

Prunus subhirtella 'Pendula'
(pru'nus sub-her-tel'-luh)
HIGAN CHERRY

Dense blossoms whirl
around the dark stems
of Yoshino cherry.

Prunus x *yedoensis* usually blooms late enough to miss the last spring frost. Huge billowing clouds of blossoms don't last long, but will cause a rush to the nursery to buy one. Its horizontal crown spreads outward to become one of the largest flowering cherries available. Fall leaf color is mild but makes an impression on dark, straight trunks and branches.

Under culture, the Yoshino cherry usually tops out at 20' tall, sometimes 30', but Dirr reminds us that it does have the capacity to go to 40 or 50'. It grows fast and quickly makes an impact. Plant with caution and be aware of the space it can eventually take up. The structural form is upright with a crown developing into a round or horizontally oval shape at maturity, more often the latter. As branches enlarge they fall closer to the ground, requiring some pruning to permit passage of lawn mowers and foot traffic. Another caution comes from Edward Gilman, in *Trees for Urban and Suburban Landscapes*; he warns that the bark is thin and easily damaged by mowers.

Trees bloom when young, so they make a show soon after being planted. Blossoms usually appear before the leaves emerge, covering the branches with such density that they cannot be seen. The flowers first appear as light pink then quickly fade white. The blossom's center is distinctively darker, giving the blossom richer color and greater depth. It is Yoshino and 'Kwanzan' cherries that create the magnificent cherry blossom festival in our nation's capital. Bark is the typically rich reddish-brown slashed with white lenticels. Small black fruits without ornamental significance ripen in June and July among dark green, serrated leaves. Cultivars include 'Akebono', with pink flowers, and 'Snow Fountains', a white, semi-weeping variety.

Full sun will ensure optimum flowering. With good drainage, a wide range of soil textures and pH will be tolerated. Judicious pruning will strengthen and enhance the architectural appeal. With its upright and spreading habit, Yoshino cherry makes a gorgeous tree for the patio or any outside area, including a street tree. The trees in the photograph are young but shapely, revealing both the pink and white stages of blossom. Dirr relates a most amazing use for this cherry as one that does "reasonably well" beneath limbed-up pines. I like it standing alone against a blue sky, or at the back of a garden, unnoticed until it becomes a large white cloud of blossom. With its upright habit, perennials can coexist nicely beneath,

Prunus x yedoensis
(pru'-nus yed-o-en'-sis)
YOSHINO CHERRY

Tall and sturdy 'Aristocrat' pears rise above an ivy-covered brick wall.

The overused Bradford pear is a structurally defective tree, inadequate in the slightest wind, likely to split in half just when it is at its peak performance. I have never used a Bradford, and it has been removed from the list of acceptable street trees by the Division of Planning in my hometown. *Pyrus calleryana* 'Aristocrat' and other more desirable forms are better trees. Dirr's favorite cultivar is 'Chanticleer'; he states that there have been fireblight problems with 'Aristocrat' in the North. I have never experienced a fireblight problem, and until growers in the Midwest make better varieties more available, 'Aristocrat' is an acceptable choice.

Aristocrats are fast-growing trees, reaching 35 to 40' in height, spreading to about 25'. There is a vertical emphasis that creates a neat, pyramidal shape with a dense canopy. Branching from a wider surface area than 'Bradford', 'Aristocrat' is stronger and safer in storms.

Blossoms are the main attraction of 'Aristocrat' in late March to early April. The pure white flowers are borne in clusters before the foliage appears, creating an unforgettable white display for about two weeks. Although the blossom period is short, it is intense, the heavy display remaining memorable as the dark green leaves appear and smother the last remaining blossoms. An added attraction in the fall is an intense red foliage color as memorable as spring's white display. Tiny brownish fruit clings to the branches long after the leaves are gone, attracting birds.

'Aristocrat' pear will tolerate inhospitable soils of different textures, low to high pH levels, drought and, as Gilman states in *Trees for Urban and Suburban Landscapes,* even some salt. 'Aristocrat' and 'Chanticleer' make good trees for the garden because they can be limbed up to accommodate underplantings of perennials or shrubs. Their vertical emphasis makes them good as a dominant structural interest for the garden, softening an expanse of wall or creating a backdrop for companionable shrubs. Both are better street trees than 'Bradford', because they have more wind resistance, and are tall and dense enough to create good shade for patios and lower decks. Both thrive in urban situations, giving excellent color in spring and fall.

Pyrus calleryana
'Aristocrat'
(pi'-rus kal-er-e-a'-nuh)
ARISTOCRAT PEAR

Rhododendrons and azaleas belong to the same genus: Rhododendron. The basic difference is that rhododendrons usually have larger and thicker leaves than azaleas. In terms of design, they create a bolder or denser presence. The hybrid groups I list in the following pages are the select, small number that I have found to be reliable enough to thrive in the Midwest. To identify a proven variety, just look around any given neighborhood and note the larger, older plants. Or, if you are lucky enough to have a botanic garden close by, go there to ask questions.

Rhododendrons & Azaleas

empting, to say the least, are the breathtaking closeups of rhododendron blossoms in garden catalogs and on nursery I.D. tags. But pretty pictures are no guarantee of performance. As gardeners, we need to know the plant's hardiness, its size at maturity, and its cultural requirements in order to determine if it is correct for our situation. Without that information, caution is called for.

The foremost requirement for success with rhododendrons is good drainage. No amount of amending the soil will substitute. If proper drainage is in doubt I usually discourage using rhododendrons, but when a client persists, I raise the plant to a higher level than the surrounding ground to help improve the drainage. Rhododendrons also need constant moisture, acidic soil, and a cool location. This can be difficult in the Midwest where hot, humid summers can take their toll on rhodos and wet winters and springs can find them with soggy feet. The pH should be between 5 and 6; any higher and the leaves will respond with chlorosis. Organic matter in the form of peat and compost helps with moisture retention. A little peat moss or fine pine bark in the hole at planting time will help increase acidity. The extra organic matter will also encourage better drainage. As a rule, rhododendrons come in containers and are rootbound. To ensure that the roots can penetrate the surrounding soil, slice the root ball vertically in several places around the root mass.

After planting, moisture retention can be increased by adding a 4" layer of pine bark mulch to cover the ground around the roots and out to the foliage line. A fine pine bark or pea gravel mixed with the soil will help with drainage and create necessary air space for the absorption of oxygen. The coolest locations are usually eastern or northern facing or under tree canopies. Rhododendrons look wonderful under trees, where shade gives ideal protection from summer heat. Direct sun and southern exposures are to be avoided at all costs.

Also avoid windy locations. I like to tuck rhododendrons in alcoves and corners, against walls and buildings, where they will benefit from reflected warmth in the winter. An application of Wilt-pruf on the foliage is good practice to insure winter survival. Wilt-pruf reduces transpiration during the cold months, thus preventing dessication from wind and sun.

Azalea 'Corsage' in a many-layered planting around a Japanese garden house at the Missouri Botanical Garden.

In the midwest, the most frequently used and reliable azaleas have been the Glenn Dale hybrids. 'Cascade' and 'Delaware Valley' have proven themselves time and again. The past few years have seen the Girard hybrids, with their improved bud hardiness, being used more and more. Gables are listed by Dirr as some of the best evergreen azaleas for Zone 5. There is no way to touch on all the azalea selections and cultivars in existence, so I will stick to ones I have used and mention others only briefly. Do visit specialty nurseries like Springhouse Gardens in Lexington, Kentucky and Lakeview Nursery in Fairfield, Ohio, and try some new and better hybrids. Both of these nurseries carry the Gable hybrid 'Karen'.

Azaleas come in all sizes. Some of the Girards range from 3 x 3' to 5 x 6'. 'Cascade' can become 4 x 6'. 'Girard's Scarlet' is 2 x 3', spreading wider than tall, which is the usual formation. These are considered evergreen because they retain their foliage throughout the winter. When in bloom, a large number of azaleas planted together is unforgettable. From April to May in the Lower Midwest, depending upon the weather, they can dominate the garden. Colors can be chosen to brighten the landscape with 2 to 3" diameter blossoms that command attention.

Ideal conditions include cool, moist weather and acidic soil. Although such conditions do not abound, azaleas, especially the Glenn Dale hybrids, can be used effectively if protected from extreme summer and winter conditions. Plenty of humus is required to maintain adequate moisture and nutrition. A 3" layer of pine bark mulch should be used to help with acidity and retain moisture. The Glenn Dales can withstand higher soil pH, so great efforts at soil preparation are not so crucial. Moisture should be maintained weekly through a drought and perhaps extra mulch applied. Pruning, if any, should be done in early spring.

In the hot summer months azaleas always fare better with some shade. They can be planted under large, deep-rooted trees so that there is adequate depth of soil, or in eastern and northern facing positions when they do not have the advantage of overhead shade. A woodland planting is ideal. Azaleas are good companions for other shrubs also, their shapes and flowers making a pleasing contrast with dwarf conifers, boxwoods, and yews. The pink and white varieties are especially nice with *Acer* 'Bloodgood' as seen in the photograph, taken in April in the Missouri Botanical Garden's Japanese Garden.

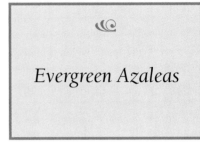

Evergreen Azaleas

'Roseum Elegans' rhododendron in an island of English
ivy under a river birch.

Out of all the thousands of rhododendrons in existence, this one puts on the strongest show for our area. One of the oldest native cultivars in use, it remains one of the most impressive when in bloom. Although others may have larger flowers, actual performance can be inferior. But 'Roseum Elegans' is dependable in both sub-zero climates and hot ones. Some of the best specimens I have seen were sheltered from both the harsh sun of Midwest summers and winters and the cold winds of winter.

When mature, 'Roseum Elegans' can become 10' in an oval to rounded shape. Short and dumpy when younger, its dense mass of foliage is usually taller than wide at maturity. Branching will spread from ground level upward, creating a solid mass of foliage.

Buds develop in late summer and fall of the previous year and are carried through the winter. If winter does not destroy them (it takes an usually harsh winter), the large, triangular trumpet-shaped flowers are impressive in May and June. Spherical clusters of lilac-purple flowers top each stem in a spectacular show. The foliage is impressive, like large, elliptical, olive-green fan blades, whirling around thick stems. In cold winters the leaves will roll up into long tubes for protection.

R. catawbiense can be affected by all the problems mentioned in the introduction, but 'Roseum Elegans' is one of the most adaptable in less than ideal locations.

'Roseum Elegans' is a good broadleaf evergreen for many places in the garden. If the lilac-pink blossoms are not attractive to you, try 'Roseum Pink', another Catawba cultivar, with soft pink trusses of blossoms in mid-May. These two are hardy to −25 degrees, and elegant enough to place next to the house or in any other highly visible area for color, structure, and contrast. They do well under trees to soften their abrupt height and to create a woodland effect. They are good companions for shady perennials like spring anemones, phlox, sweet woodruff, and many others. With other shrubs, rhododendrons can be the evergreen anchor. One of their best attributes is the way they can create interest in shady areas. Good ground companions are arums, ferns, hostas, *Phlox divaricata*, spring bulbs, and astilbes.

Rhododendron catawbiense
'Roseum Elegans'
(ro-do-den'-dron ka-taw-bi-en'-see)
CATAWBA RHODODENDRON

One of the brighter Exbury azaleas bringing life into an otherwise all-green part of the garden. Located at the northeast corner of the house, it tolerates clay-based soil. An ample layer (3–4") of small pine bark mulch increases moisture retention. This particular azalea is growing in a bed of pachysandra ground cover, with companions of bergenia, 'Hoopsii' blue spruce, and *Iris pseudacorus* (yellow flag iris). The evergreen azalea 'Delaware Valley' covers the base of the taller, sparse-branching deciduous azalea.

These distinctive azaleas with an extensive range of cultivars in intense colors appear leafless in the spring. The leaves are there, but the blossoms dominate, giving them a striking and exotic appearance. If these brighter colors are too much, there are some hybrids softened with cream. There are literally hundreds to choose from—some with an attractive upright habit, some with fragrant blossoms, and others that display new bronze foliage to complement the flowers. They vary from 8' to 12' tall and from 2' to 3' wide. They branch openly with thin dark branches and appear top-heavy when in bloom. Shorter cultivars like 'Wallow Red' are 4–8' tall and 3–5' wide.

Flowers as large as 5" need no help to attract attention, yet some also reach out with tropical colors, captivating the viewer. Most hybrids have smaller, modest blossom sizes of 2½", but the vibrant colors more than make up for the smaller size. They range from pure white, bright oranges, and reds to blends with pink and cream. The blossoms cluster at the end of the branches. 'Doctor Rudolf Henny' has 10 flowers per cluster, some with frilled or ruffled petals. Apricot-peach blossoms come on 'Cacatoo', a Knap Hill hybrid. One of the more commonly sold in our area is the heat-tolerant 'Gibraltar', another Knap Hill, with hot-orange blossoms. While some of these hybrids have exciting blossom color and some are flower hardy to –24 degrees, care must be taken to assure that local nursery selections are hardy specifically for the Midwest. Acknowledged hardiness is listed as from Zone 5 to Zone 7. I have used 'Gibraltar', 'Klondyke', 'Peachy Keen', and 'Exbury White' with success. These are a mere handful of the hundreds available. For further information about heat and cold tolerant deciduous azaleas, I refer you to the catalog of Fairweather Gardens in New Jersey. Like all rhododendrons, deciduous azaleas require an acidic, moist soil and an eastern facing location or filtered shade.

Woodland settings tend to provide the shade and moisture requirements necessary for success with deciduous azaleas, as well for a base array of companionable perennials and shrubs. One precaution to keep in mind is color combinations. While the blue background of the spruce is pleasing with the azalea in the photograph, it might not be with a purple companion of 'PJM' rhododendron. Let your imagination and color preferences do the color blending to be sure that your azaleas are compatible with other shrubs when grouped together.

Deciduous Azaleas

This 'PJM' rhododendron brightens a corner under a dogwood and in front of a viburnum. Cultural requirements for the Mezitt/Weston hybrids are listed in the introduction to this section. Just remember that their shallow, fibrous roots need to be kept moist.

'PJM' is the proverbial "tip of the iceberg" among some of the hardiest rhododendrons ever developed—the Mezitt/Weston hybrids. With parents like the Carolina rhododendron (*R. carolinianum*) and the Dahurian (*R. dauricum*) from the mountains of northern Japan, it is no wonder they are hardy and vigorous. All have a small stature, with a good round shape that makes them attractive where larger rhododendrons would be overbearing. Thanks to the work of Edmund Mezitt of Weston Nurseries, Hopkinton, Massachusetts, we have a large selection to choose from. Leaves are petite for a rhododendron. Nevertheless, they are evergreen, vigorous, and the best to use after *R. catawbiense* types.

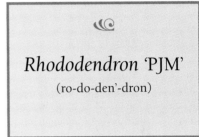

Rhododendron 'PJM'
(ro-do-den'-dron)

Most of the Mezitt/Weston hybrids mature to between 6' and 8', making them more compact. It is difficult to generalize, because smaller ones like 'Milestone', a pink-budded variety, attain only 3' after ten years. The plants are densely branched, with an even, rounded form.

Blossoms come early in the season on 'PJM', a vivid lavender-pink, from mid to late April. Given a warm October, 'PJM' will rebloom. Flowering is heavy in the spring, sparse in the fall. Leaves are small dark green during the growing season, only 1" to 2" long, and will turn different shades of red in autumn, depending upon which hybrid is chosen. 'Balta' is a slow growing compact plant with pale pink flowers, 'Olga Mezitt' a pink blended with peach.

I have always wanted to see a very large grouping of PJMs closely associated with a specimen of *Prunus subhirtella* 'Autumnalis', just to witness their late fall blossoms together. The combination of the cherry's light pink and the rhododendron's lavender-purple would be delightful. PJMs are bold in color and should be boldly used. Often you will see one lone specimen in a foundation planting, whereas three would be more effective. In larger spaces, consider a grouping of five or more.

Other good blooming partners would be amelanchiers, such as 'Autumn Brilliance' and 'Cumulus'. Rhododendrons in any of the colors mentioned above will make a nice skirt for the taller amelanchiers and at the same time wed the two together. A planting of perennials beneath the rhododendrons could include *Ajuga* 'Bronze Beauty' and *Myosotis sylvatica*, for complementary colors, or *Liriope spicata* for an interesting textural contrast. Any of the ground covers would effectively anchor all elements (sky, tree, and shrub) together.

Roses

oses can be endlessly fascinating. In addition to being colorful, they climb (with some help), create living arches, cover unsightly walls, and add fragrance. Some, such as 'Zephirine Drouhin', will perform as large shrubs or climbers. Others, like 'Frau Dagmar Hartopp', bloom with a flourish in the spring and then sporadically the rest of the season.

I was fortunate to have started out with a concept of a well-balanced garden, with roses as an integral part but not the total domination and focus of it. To this day I tend to mix roses with annuals, perennials, shrubs, and trees in my design work. A rose garden sounds romantic but involves a great amount of care and the willingness to contaminate onself and the environment with the sprays necessary to keep the foliage in pristine condition. The best way to avoid harmful chemicals is to select roses that are relatively trouble free and then keep them healthy (see Maggie Oster's *Rose Book*). An attitude adjustment on the part of the gardener may also be advisable: a certain amount of blackspot can be tolerated. The same goes for thrips, spider mites, and so on.

My favorite way to install roses is bare root, in the late fall or winter. I prune the canes back to three in a fan shape. Next I prune the roots about a fifth and remove any that might be defective, spraying my pruners with alcohol between plants to prevent the spread of disease. This is imperative for healthy roses. Whenever moving from rose to rose, whether it be during planting or general maintenance pruning, I always spray my shears with alcohol.

To insure that a rose begins life properly, combine organic matter with the existing soil and place the crown 2" below ground level. Compost is the preferred organic matter; chop up the existing soil and mix with bonemeal, alfalfa pellets, or both at planting time. Make sure the hole is large enough for the roots to spread out freely, mixing the ingredients with the soil until the hole is filled. Tamp the soil firmly around the roots to remove any air spaces. Water generously to help settle the plant. After planting, I usually spread a rose fertilizer as top dressing, or use a 10-10-10, all-purpose fertilizer. Most of the following roses will succeed with only one feeding in the early spring. Water liberally if there is no rain.

Besides the initial pruning, I keep the canes on the inside of the bush thinned, and cut above outer-facing eyes to encourage outward growth. Dead branches should of course be removed.

Roses, above: 'Alchymist'; facing page, above: 'New Dawn'; below, 'Zephirine Drouhin' with 'Silver Moon'. As a general rule, repeat bloomers should be pruned in the winter or very early spring. Those that only bloom once can be pruned after flowering.

'New Dawn', running across a guest house, has been known as an impressive climber for seventy years. 'Zephirine Drouhin' is on the arbor.

One of my first recommendations for a disease-resistant rambler is always *Rosa x alba* 'New Dawn'. 'New Dawn' has been listed as a repeat bloomer since its introduction in 1930 by the Somerset Rose Nursery. Tom Christopher, in *Easy Roses for North American Gardens,* says that it caused such a stir when introduced that it gained the first plant patent ever issued in the U.S. Once established, 'New Dawn' characteristically sends out branches that are long and graceful. There is no "carefree" climber, because roses have to be trained to a support, but 'New Dawn' is as close as a climber can come to being trouble free.

The height of this 'Dr. Van Fleet' sport was supposedly reduced to 10' but as you see in the photograph, can be closer to 20', like its parent. If no effort is made to control them, most climbers, including 'New Dawn', will naturally sprawl or wallow; the neat word "climber" was invented to counteract that unattractive image. Thick, sturdy canes sprout dark red thorns that are produced from a hardy, vigorous root stock.

The thick, glossy, dark-green foliage is the perfect foil for the lush, shell-pink semidouble blossoms, which are opulent in bud as well as when unfurling. When fully opened, there is a show of bright gold stamens and a sweet fragrance. Clusters form at the terminal end of every branch, making one lone stem a cut-flower bouquet all by itself.

If the above characteristics do not sufficiently impress, maybe its capable disposition will. Tough cultural conditions do not slow it down, making it one of the most carefree and disease-free roses I have ever used. It tolerates most soil conditions, contracting very little blackspot or other disease. The only problem I have seen with it in fifteen years was an infestation of spider mites during the drought year of 1999. Even this was not enough to make the rose look bad. Plant as suggested in the introduction. Prune old wood and canes back to the desired boundaries after the first great flush of blossom in June.

'New Dawn' can be displayed to best advantage at the top of a 4' to 5' retaining wall where, given its tendency to sprawl, it will flow beautifully over the wall. Or train it up into a tree and let it cascade back down. Or it can be trained as you see it in the photograph. Tied to a strong trellis on a modest guest house, it has been an attraction for fifteen years. It could just as well ramble right over and up onto the roof if lattice were provided. It can be used as a shrub or a hedge, but I think it is better as a rambling climber on a fence or trellis, or running over a stone wall.

Rosa x alba
'New Dawn'
(ro'-za all-buh')

If left to spread naturally, 'Zephirine Drouhin' can become a veritable mountain of blossoms. And it will never punish the passerby who leans in to smell or pick a blossom, for it is thornless.

'Zephirine Drouhin', popular ever since its introduction in 1868 by Bizot of France, is an astonishing rose. Fragrant and hardy, it blooms profusely in spring and early summer, then sporadically throughout the season. I have used it since 1985, when the only source was Pickering Nurseries in Canada. (I still order from them, and find no better roses anywhere. See Resources.)

Grown as a shrub, the branches will become 15' or longer, which means it will spread that wide; but as the canes elongate they fall over, reducing the height to an overall 8-10'. Its branches cascade densely, making a thick blanket, sprouting secondary growth at every node segment along their descent. The canes, which have deep burgundy foliage when new, grow straight upward, then gracefully fall over.

Sweet smelling, semi-double carmine flowers cover this rose in small clusters, first teasing the gardener in late May. The greatest flush of bloom is in June, but it repeats until frost, making it worthy of applause. What better complement to the pink blossoms than foliage emerging bright copper-red, then slowly fading to a bright, dark green?

One of the easier roses to use in the garden, 'Zephirine Drouhin' has such vigor that it will tolerate hostile situations as long as it has a sunny location. A testament to this amazing vigor is the plant in the photograph, which was never set into the ground. For five years it has been growing out of a nursery pot in hard-packed, yellow clay, with no effort on my part. The inhospitable soil does have good drainage. It was not always so large (the roots did have to grow through the container), but it has bloomed every year. It is rarely sprayed and consequently does contract blackspot after its heavy blooming period, but I do not go into attack mode unless I think all the foliage is in danger. It seldom is. The plant is so large, I can discourage blackspot by pruning and discarding any affected branches. This pruning only encourages new growth. Other than shaping, removal of dead wood is the only pruning necessary.

'Zephirine Drouhin' is trouble-free falling from the top of a retaining wall, which at the same time highlights its gracious, natural form. A small hill or slight decline, a fence or a berm will also do. It does make a good climber with considerably more effort and a strong support. Arbors, pergolas, and walls are good supportive structures. Being thornless, it is user-friendly for heavy-traffic areas. Definitely large enough to hold its own in association with trees and shrubs, it can be an asset for any garden—if there is space.

Rosa x borboniana
'Zephirine Drouhin'
BOURBON CLIMBER

A variegated shrub dogwood and rose 'Fantin-Latour' spilling over a retaining wall, creating a scented sitting area.

The date and parentage of *Rosa* 'Fantin-Latour' are not known, but it was named after the French artist Henri Fantin-Latour (1836–1904), who was noted for his paintings of floral arrangements. This is another shrub rose of great stature that grows with a vertical emphasis. It blooms only once, but that is forgiven because the abundant blossoms have rich pink petals with the characteristic centifolia fragrance.

'Fantin-Latour' has an upright habit of 5', with a spread as wide if given the space it needs. It branches thickly from the crown, forming an inverted pyramidal shape in full sun. I have one at the top of a retaining wall facing south that cascades downward, reaching for the light. It makes a stronger shrub, becoming graceful over the years as its branches spill over like a fountain. It is thickly branched, with dense, rich green foliage thought to be influenced by the China rose, as David Austin explains in *The Heritage of the Rose.*

Although the flower is the main attraction, the foliage of this old rose makes a perfect gray-green background. June flowers begin as dark pink buds, forming dense cups as they mature, with lower petals reflexing when open. A mature blossom is 4" to 5" in diameter and clear pink, displaying the typical centifolia density when fully open. The fragrance is delicately sweet and aromatic when brought inside the house.

If given full-sun exposure and good drainage, 'Fantin-Latour' tolerates different soil types and flourishes in difficult situations. Vigorous growth and tenacity are other endearing qualities. Feed regularly like other roses, and prune after it blooms. The only fault I have found with 'Fantin-Latour' is its propensity for blackspot in open, windy situations.

'Fantin-Latour' has the size to anchor other plantings, although I would not use it in a highly visible area. A better placement would be against a fence or stationed beside other shrubs of a similar height, such as *Spiraea* 'Snowmound' or a large boxwood, where the characteristically bare lower canes can be hidden. It would be a fountain-like statue planted among perennials. The branches are long enough to let it be a small climber, espaliered on a wall.

Rosa x centifolia
'Fantin-Latour'

Lush 'Alchymist' trained to
a wooden tripod behind a
row of boxwood.

One of the better pink blends, derived from a cross between a dark pink species rose and a yellow hybrid tea. Usually described as apricot or coral, 'Alchymist' is always impressive when blooming. It has the scent and rosette petals of Old World roses and the vigor of a shrub or climber. 'Alchymist' only blooms once but is magnificent when it does. It goes back to 1956, when it was introduced by Kordes of Germany, and takes some work to tame, but the reward is a delicious rose.

Some list this as a 6' shrub. I cannot imagine why. It becomes 8' to 12' in most of the Midwest, except maybe the cooler upper regions of Zone 5. Unless it is severely chopped into submission, it will sprawl over everything nearby. As seen in the photograph, it can best be used on a vertical pillar or in other situations that take advantage of its long canes.

The flower is tightly constructed in an old-fashioned way, with double petals and a strong fragrance. A close look reveals the darker apricot center, swirling into four or five distinct lobes, the lower petals pinker and curling under slightly. There is one heavy show of blossoms in May to June, depending upon its location. Warmer winters will encourage more blossoms the following spring. Glossy foliage is thick and dark green.

This is not a choice rose if you cannot stand blackspot or mind spraying fungicides. It succumbs to blackspot in rural, windy areas more than in urban sites. It must have full sun, with the infected leaves picked off the canes weekly and any fallen leaves cleaned off the ground. Spreading sulfur around the base of the plant helps control the spread of blackspot too. Rather than spray constantly, I let the lower canes become bare of leaves and simply rely upon a taller screen to hide them from view.

One of its best uses is seen in the photograph: tied to an 8' tripod, securely sunk into the ground about a foot. This and other wooden rose supports are easily explained in *Basic Projects and Plantings*. Such supports can be placed throughout the garden among perennials to vary height or in a row to create a background wall. My other favorite way to display 'Alchymist' is hanging over a retaining wall. Planting at the top of the wall shows the canes to best advantage, without the work of training them on a support. Other easy situations would be in a large area for it to sprawl, next to a wall to fall over, or beside a tree that will support the canes as they grow upward. I like it planted with shrubs at the base because the lower canes tend to become bare with age.

Rosa 'Alchymist'
CLIMBER

'Sally Holmes' is the perfect repeating climber for a fence.

One of my favorite, best all-around, problem-free roses. I was at first skeptical when a client came back from England raving about its beauty, but soon found it in a reference work and liked the look of the single blossoms. This combined with an all-season flowering period led me to decide I would try it. I remained skeptical until I found a source and had one in the ground. That was a few years ago, and since then 'Sally Holmes' has proven itself in our brutal climate.

Shrub or climber, 'Sally Holmes' has the capacity to reach 7–10'. It is often claimed that it is smaller, but the plants I have ordered have all been on the taller end, probably because they have been grafted onto a different rootstock. In colder climates, it remains closer to 5'. It is a slow starter when purchased on its own roots and needs two years to begin strong growth. This is another rose I have difficulty using as a shrub. Pruning to contain such vigor is time consuming and distracts from its natural beauty.

Pale, peachy buds begin forming large trusses of tightly packed clusters in early to mid-May, emerging in a flush of single, 4" pinkish-ivory blossoms. New stems supporting the blossom clusters are red, with dark green leaves. Blossoms open cup-shaped, then spread symmetrically flat, showing off golden stamens, tipped by tiny mahogany anthers. Resting after the first great flush of blossoms, 'Sally Holmes' carries a light fragrance and continues flowering all season until heavy frost.

I have grown this rose in clay soil with very little effort except the pruning of dead branches and the tying up of canes. In full sun, blackspot is not troublesome. I have not encountered a susceptibility to any other common rose diseases in a period of seven years. The yearly feeding is done once in early spring. A strong trellis is advisable to support the heavy canes of maturity.

If you are an admirer of single or white roses, you should have this one. Regardless of color, 'Sally Holmes' is one of the very few roses I continue to depend upon. The best uses are on a fence, as seen in the photo, against a flat surface, such as a house wall, or on an arbor. The ivory blossoms blend with the colors of such other plants as achillea and campanula. I also like to plant a blue clematis at the base of this rose and let it ramble up through the white blossoms.

Rosa 'Sally Holmes'

CLIMBER

The vigorous 'Silver Moon' spreading 15' wide and 12' tall, growing naturally over a wall. Beside it is 'Zephirine Drouhin'.

A rose of enormous vigor, *Rosa* 'Silver Moon' grows up to 30', its exuberance discovered by Dr. W. Van Fleet. *RR. laevigata* and *wichuraiana* are the suspected parents. Since 1910, 'Silver Moon' has impressed gardeners with its glossy foliage, single flowers, and fruity fragrance. This is a splendid rose to use for quick results even though it only blooms once, in midseason.

The size of this rose can be restricted only by spending hours pruning back the long canes, so it needs proper placement. Once in the ground it grows quickly, a dense mass of thorny canes. It takes about five years to become the thick, sprawling shrub you see in the photograph. Ultimately, it stands about 8' to 10' tall after the canes fall over with mature weight.

The flowers are pure white, 4-6" in diameter, and mostly semi-double. Flower clusters are held in large trusses of 8 to 24 buds, covering the plant in late May to June. Blossoms only come once a year but are abundant and sensational as they form a wall of white. The foliage maintains a healthy glow all season with its dark green and glossy surface.

Culture could not be easier. After planting in plenty of sun, there is little to do. My own 'Silver Moon', in hard yellow clay, remains good looking with virtually no feeding or spraying. Even when its companion, 'Zephirine Drouhin', begins showing blackspot, 'Silver Moon' does not contract enough to bother with. The two can be seen together in the featured photograph. During the drought of 1999 here in Lexington, I watered once a month, but that was only to keep the plant healthy.

'Silver Moon' will grow big enough to screen unsightly views. It will grow up and over a fence without much effort, although a strong trellis would be beneficial in the beginning. Unless used in its natural form, as the photograph demonstrates, some kind of support will be necessary. I recommend stretching heavy-gauge copper wire between brass eye-hooks, on any flat surface, to provide a good start and support the weight of the plant in the future. I like blending the white blossoms of 'Silver Moon' with other roses like 'Alchymist' or 'Zephirine Drouhin' to enhance their color. It would grow effortlessly up and over an arbor, and make a good host for clematis too.

Rosa 'Silver Moon'

CLIMBER

The beautiful salmon-pink 'Lilian Austin' makes a great shrub rose if given sufficient space.

'Lilian Austin' is from the great English hybridizer David Austin. Austin himself, in *The Heritage of the Rose,* describes it as "a first class garden shrub." Its brilliant color is stunning. It repeat-blooms all season after a prolific burst in mid-May. The flowers cluster at the ends of the arching branches, glowing as if lighted from within.

'Lilian Austin' is indeed a wonderful shrub, attaining a height and width of 5', forming a nice round, cascading shape. Catalogs list it at 4' but I find that Midwest heat must cause it to become taller—it could not be the rich soil. This rose flourishes in adverse soil, getting little blackspot, and continues to bloom without pause. The plant is covered with 6" salmon-pink blossoms that are richly semi-double. The individual flowers have undulating petals with yellow at the center, with rich fragrance. As new blossoms appear, the older blossoms fade to a light pink. Foliage is thick and dark green, dressing the plant throughout the season.

As a movie star thrives on publicity, 'Lilian Austin' thrives in clay soils—with unmistakable aplomb, as witnessed in the photograph. It is disease resistant, given a sunny location. It will contract some blackspot, but, once again, not enough to disfigure the entire shrub. Removing infected foliage from the plant and keeping it picked up off the ground will go a long way toward reducing blackspot.

In the photograph, 'Lilian Austin' is standing next to a *Buddleia davidii* 'Black Knight'. They do not bloom together, but because of the contrasting foliage they make an interesting pair. Choose shrubs of similar height, such as *Spiraea nipponica* 'Snowmound', to share in a mixed shrub planting, or smaller shrubs such as *Hydrangea arborescens* 'Annabelle' for contrast. This is also a good rose to use in perennial beds to add relief both in color and height. A large planting of Russian sage would make a good blue and white companion.

Rosa 'Lilian Austin'

ENGLISH ROSE

'Sun Flare', one of the best floribunda roses ever.

I consider this yellow beauty one of the top five roses. I will not use the deceptive word "carefree," but "problem-free" comes close. The most I do to this rose in an average season is to keep the old blossoms clipped off. It tolerates troublesome soils and extreme heat and continues to bloom until a hard freeze. If you have not tried this little gem, you are missing out on one of the best roses offered today.

'Sun Flare' is a small, vigorous shrub of 2' to 3', more tall than wide. Individual stems grow upward from the crown, forming an open-branched bush, spreading slowly as it ages and never becoming very dense. Thick, dark green leaves characterize the foliage that accentuates the yellow blossoms. 'Sun Flare' is hardy, but I always cover the crown with six inches of mulch in the winter.

Flowering begins in late May to early June as rich yellow buds, held on upright stems of multiple clusters, offering a light fragrance. Blossoms have double petals like a hybrid tea, only smaller. They open a canary yellow that later fades to a pale yellow. Frequent deadheading will encourage continuous flowering.

The first requirement is a full-sun location. 'Sun Flare' tolerates clay soils extremely well. It will get a little blackspot, but not enough to strip the foliage. I place the crown two inches below the ground line for stronger growth and extra winter protection. Deadheading is done weekly and feeding usually once a month.

Because it is not overwhelming in stature, 'Sun Flare' is a good rose to use with perennials—perhaps peonies, lamb's-ear, campanulas, and hardy geraniums such as 'Johnson's Blue'. In groups of three or more it will be compatible with larger shrubs, as can be seen in the photograph, where it shares space with other roses, a boxwood, and a yellow conifer. It is also effective at the outer perimeter of a group of larger shrubs to graduate their abrupt height.

Rosa floribunda
'Sun Flare'
FLORIBUNDA

'Golden Wings' in the foreground remains showy after a heavy rain. 'Alchymist' climbs the tripods in the background.

The American Rose Society Gold Medal award winner 'Golden Wings' goes back to the 1950s. To this day, it remains a great rose for the landscape. A vigorous shrub rose with upright stature and loose form, it blooms in early June and continues blooming until a freeze halts production.

'Golden Wings' attains a height of 5' and a width of 4'. It branches thickly from the base and spreads into an inverted pyramidal shape. The loose formation of canes is best kept thinned, pruned in late winter or very early spring. Foliage emerges yellow green, turning a pale green for the season, dense and disease resistant.

Subtly scented blossoms begin as light yellow buds that become 5" single flowers. Mature flowers open wide to reveal ornate, wavy petals, the upper part tipped light yellow, the lower area darkening into a primrose yellow, accented by striking orange stamens. The blooms fade to a creamy white until they fall apart. Once the first flower appears, blossoms continue until the end of the season.

'Golden Wings' is tolerant of inhospitable clay soil as long as it is in full sun. It may be longer lived in loam, but I know specimens that have lasted in clay soil for more than ten years. Although this rose is catalogued as disease resistant, a small amount of blackspot may occur, depending upon what associated plants are nearby. In windy rural areas blackspot is more prevalent than in the city. Monthly feeding is advisable, especially in clay soils, along with weekly deadheading.

'Golden Wings' is large enough to hold its own with most shrubs and stands as an anchor to other roses as seen in the photograph. Interplanted with perennials such as daylilies and peonies, and shrubs such as golden spireas, the rose will complement them all with color as well as leaf texture.

Rosa
'Golden Wings'
MODERN SHRUB ROSE

The prolific white *Rosa rugosa alba* in a sunny bed with *Iris pseudacorus* and some hybrid tea roses.

Rosa rugosa alba is number 4 on my favorite-roses list for gardens and landscapes. There are no more than a dozen names on this list, and two are cultivars from the rugosa group. *Alba* has the best of the rugosa characteristics: large, single, fragrant flowers; coarse, textured leaves with deep veins; and a hardiness and vigor to thrive in any location, including the seashore. Among other attributes it has repeated flowering and orange-red hips.

A fast-growing shrub about 5' or 6', it spreads in a broad manner with the darkest of green foliage that is a show all by itself. I like it best as a 3-4' mound as can be seen in the photograph. New foliage is lime-green, folded tight, like little fans, as it develops, then maturing to blackish-green.

The rich color and texture of the foliage make a perfect background for the pure white 4" blossoms, which are lightly scented and have a full circle of golden yellow stamens. Buds are arranged in large clusters that begin opening in early to mid-June. Flowers cover the plant during the first flush of bloom, then continue until the first freeze. Let the early flowers mature on the plant and they will develop into beautiful orange-red hips. Successive blossoms will accompany these bright hips and together make for a rare, exhilarating display of color. Unlike most roses, *R. rugosa alba* does not stop with white blooms and showy rose hips. Its fall foliage turns yellow when cold temperatures come, a delightful addition to the mix of red hips and white blossoms.

I would not hesitate to try *alba* anywhere there was a sunny position. It is hands down one of the toughest and prettiest roses for the garden. Its vigor is unmatched in the rose kingdom, and it is one of the only roses that could be truly labeled carefree. Except for aphids, nothing seems to bother the two rugosa roses I use, and I suggest their use at every possible opportunity. *R. rugosa alba* is a must in a "white garden" and because of its size will give needed structure to any landscape. The white blossoms blend and soften all other colors in a perennial border or mixed shrub arrangement. In the photograph, two albas anchor the corner of a rose garden, separating the lawn from the rose beds.

Rosa rugosa alba

The best landscape rose ever
is tough as nails and keeps
on blooming: 'Frau Dagmar
Hartopp'.

This is number 1 on my list of best roses. It is a true carefree rose. Compact and bushy, *R. r.* 'Frau Dagmar Hartopp' ('Fru Dagmar Hastrup') is an elegant small shrub that will tolerate just about anything. I have never had to spray for any disease or blackspot. I have never seen it in a local nursery either, but it is readily available by mail order (see Resources).

'Frau Dagmar' is a robust shrub about 4 x 4', known for its ability to remain smaller than other rugosas. It is easily kept smaller if required. I like to shape it into a mound about 3' x 4'. The one in the photograph is kept at those dimensions to stay in proportion with the surrounding shrubs and sidewalk perimeter.

The flowers of 'Frau Dagmar' are single, tissue thin, and a rich medium pink. At 4" in diameter with a light scent, they are impressive. Blossoms begin as tightly curled clusters of five or more, held on apple-green stems, every inch covered with thorns. Dark pink buds are long teardrops, wrapped with pointed, lime-green sepals. Buds open with cupped petals, turning a lighter pink as they unfold and mature, revealing pale yellow stamens arranged in a star-like pattern. The heaviest truss of blossoms begins in late May to June, while a smaller amount continues through frost. Like *alba*, 'Frau Dagmar' will develop large, dark red hips in the fall, resembling miniature apples.

Tolerance of clay soils, summer heat, and cold wet winters makes 'Frau Dagmar' a perfect rose for the Lower Midwest and most of the United States. As long as it is placed in a sunny location, it is not particular. I would like to hear how far its northward hardiness boundaries extend. The only problem I have encountered with this rose is aphids in the early spring, which can be taken care of with a spray of insecticidal soap.

'Frau Dagmar Hartopp' can be used among other shrubs as well as with perennials. The specimen in the photograph is planted in an arrangement with *Ilex* 'Blue Princess' harmonizing in the fall with red berries and *Rosa* 'York and Lancaster', which complements it when blooming, and anchored with a boxwood on the end. This array of varied texture and form creates an interesting combination along the pool terrace. As a shrub mixed with perennials, 'Frau Dagmar' offers an interesting foundation of texture and color all season.

Rosa rugosa
'Frau Dagmar
Hartopp'

A monster rose covering twenty feet of wall space: 'Leontine Gervais'.

Rosa wichuraiana 'Leontine Gervais' is a cross between the species *R. wichuraiana* and a tea rose by Barbier of France. The result is a vigorous trailing habit, glossy foliage, and exquisite blossoms. In its native habitat of Japan and East China, *wichuraiana* rambles along the ground, climbing up anything that will give purchase. 'Leontine Gervais' is no different, needing a vast expanse of wall and plenty of support. A more dramatic pink-blended rose cannot be found.

This big rose rambles up to 25'. Densely branched with shiny, dark green foliage, it is a fast starter, running up a trellis in two or three years even when planted in difficult soil. In the photograph you can see some of the underlying wooden trellis that was used to support the first canes. After about ten feet, the higher canes are supported by more trellis made with screw-eyes and copper wire. It would go up over the house if there was support.

The blossoms are a blend of apricot and yellow with a light fragrance. Three-inch, rosy-yellow buds open with soft, double, apricot petals. Blossoms are prolific beginning in early May, reaching their peak by mid-month. The petals open loosely, with a *centifolia* character and a light yellow center. Delicate stems suspend the blossoms outward for an airy effect, enhanced by the rich, dainty leaves. Such a wonderful rose can be forgiven for blooming only once!

A negligible amount of blackspot is the only problem I have ever encountered with 'Leontine Gervais'. Once installed in a sunny location, all the work is concentrated on keeping it trained to a trellis support and restraining it from smothering other climbers sharing the same wall. The example in the photograph is situated in an eastern-facing location, doing well in sticky yellow clay. Fertilizing is done in early spring.

Arbors, fences, pergolas, and walls would all be likely subjects for 'Leontine Gervais' to cover. It would be a great rose for rambling over a stone wall. A good companion on the same wall would be 'Sally Holmes' or 'Silver Moon'. The former would extend blossom time, and the latter would intermingle with 'Leontine Gervais' for a striking combination. Another companion to twine among the apricot blossoms would be a blue or a white clematis. Covering an arbor would be easy for this rambling rose, along with variegated porcelain vine for contrast and continued attraction.

Rosa wichuraiana
'Leontine Gervais'
WICHURAIANA HYBRID

One of the few trees with bright orange berries in fall, European mountainash strikes a pose along a driveway entrance. Stunted because it grows in alkaline, compacted soil, this one has nonetheless delighted its owner for ten years. A tree does not need to perform to the maximum to be effective in the landscape.

These much-neglected trees are great ornamentals in all their aspects. With compound leaves, clustered flowers, striking berries, and fall color, both the American and the European mountainash offer distinctive features for gardens, especially those in the northern reaches of the Midwest. The European is more readily available, but either is worth locating.

Sorbus americana reaches 30' at most and grows with a short trunk and rounded crown. *S. aucuparia* reaches 20 to 40', erect in youth, developing a round crown only at maturity. Both have an open branching habit, with the American mountainash more vertically conspicuous. It is hardy to Zone 2, *S. aucuparia* to Zone 3.

White, flat-topped blossom clusters with a musty odor first appear in late April to early May. They are a welcome sight, but more effective is the brilliant fruit that later hangs from the branches. Berries are bright orange to dark red, with some *aucuparia* hybrids offering yellow and one even pink fruit. Even the small amount of fruit visible in the photograph demonstrates its vivid color. Both trees have pinnately compound leaves, the American slightly longer, the European with more leaflets per leaf, and serrated edges beginning higher from the basal stem. Color does not stop with the fruit. In fall the leaves turn yellow, then orange-red to scarlet.

Mountainash thrives in well-drained soils of good loam and high acidity, and in full sun. More adaptable than it is given credit for, it is showy even under harsh conditions. Although it is not the best tree for hotter regions—intense heat will stunt its growth—it can be effective for many years. Sweet and compacted soils tend to stress the tree, making it susceptible to canker and borers. If planted in a clay-based soil, a yearly feeding with nutritionally balanced tree spikes is recommended.

Its all-season appeal makes mountainash a candidate for highly visible placement. Against a backdrop of dark fencing or summer foliage, it shows to best advantage. In early morning light, suffused with high humidity, as seen in the photograph, the foliage takes on a hazy blue cast. Also good, either as background or nearby companions, are blue spruces or red Japanese maples, depending upon one's personal color preference. In the shade of larger trees, and located on the eastern side of buildings, mountainash will be screened from the harsh midday sun. Underplantings of perennials and traditional groundcovers can thrive if the lower branches are raised, letting sufficient light reach them. Another good complementary shrub is 'Snowmound' spirea, blooming in white profusion along with the tree.

Sorbus americana,
Sorbus aucuparia
(sor'-bus a-mer'-i-cana,
au'-kew-pah'-ria)
MOUNTAINASH, ROWAN TREE

A hot but good companion with white Sargent crab and a globe blue spruce is 'Goldmound' spirea.

Two small spireas with a hardy and undemanding nature are *Spiraea x japonica* 'Goldmound' and *S. x japonica* 'Shibori'. Both are good for contrasting and brightening any garden view, 'Shibori' ('Shirobana') with tricolor flowers all season on the same plant, 'Goldmound' with distinctive foliage that can accent the garden, somewhat like using a yellow highlighter. Walking through the garden, even on a cloudy day, you cannot miss its bright face. These are the two plants I always think of for adding contrast, with either foliage or flowers, among perennials, shrubs, and trees.

'Goldmound' is compact, as its name implies, mounding about 3 x 4' into a broad, even shape. 'Shibori' manages a 2–3' mound. Both readily accept pruning if you want to keep them smaller. Each has petite, serrated foliage, the former bright yellow and the latter lustrous, bright green, both densely arranged on reddish-brown stems. The leaves of 'Goldmound' emerge in the spring an intense yellow, then change to a golden yellow for the summer. 'Shibori' provides early attraction in the garden by initiating its leaves earlier than most spireas.

Small clusters of rosy-pink flowers cover the golden foliage of 'Goldmound' in June, while 'Shibori' blooms in the same month with flower clusters of rose, pink, and white—some clusters carrying all three flower colors. If you find the pink blossoms of 'Goldmound' unsettling with its yellow foliage, the flowers can easily be sheared away. 'Shibori' does not present this problem. Its impressive flowers bloom sporadically throughout the season.

Spireas in general are very tolerant of different soil types. They prefer more acidic soils, but grow in any moist situation that drains well. They tolerate short dry periods in the Midwest, as well as proving themselves adaptable in alkaline and clay-based soil. Both do their best where they receive full sun. If there is ever any winter damage or reshaping necessary, either can be cut down to the ground in late winter or very early spring. Aphids have been the only problem in an otherwise trouble-free shrub, and they are easily taken care of with insecticidal soap.

In the illustration, 'Goldmound' enhances an island planting. I also like to use 'Goldmound' for colorful relief among green shrubs by placing them at appropriate intervals, either singly or threes. The foliage of both can brighten and introduces a colorful contrast amongst perennials, roses and other shrubs too. Use the smaller 'Shibori' to anchor a group of perennials and/or as partners for *Buxus* 'Green Gem' and 'Green Mound'. Both serve to balance the scene with similar forms of different colors.

Spiraea x japonica
(spi-re'-ah ja-pon'-i-kuh)
JAPANESE SPIREA

'Snowmound' spirea is a good shrub to face down taller trees, such as the Foster's hollies seen here.

No landscape should be without this beautiful shrub. It is my favorite spirea, not only because of its prolific bloom but for the all-season bluish-green foliage it carries in a good round shape. 'Snowmound' is reliable and as trouble free as a shrub can be in the garden or planted in large urns.

'Snowmound' grows into a tight, rounded form about 5 x 5', its soft, blue-green leaves an asset long after the blossoms have faded. If permitted to grow naturally the plant will become an elegant spray of white arching branches when it blooms. Closely cropped shrubs have their place, but 'Snowmound' does not look good tightly sheared. If a shorter height is required it is best to prune the entire shrub. Older branches will sometimes die out, but even in fifteen-year-old plants I have not seen enough dieback to disfigure a plant. If the loss of many such branches causes an unsightly openness, cut the entire shrub back to 18" to 2' and start over.

Flowers usually begin to appear in early May, peak about mid-month, and continue for another two weeks. In the photograph, they can be seen displayed in their natural spiky sprays. These arching branches are a good source for flower and foliage for cut arrangements.

Spireas like moist soil and full sun and will tolerate shade. I have had great results in a variety of soil types; the photographed example grows in clay. A 4" layer of mulch will help with moisture retention. Their vigor and versatility are unsurpassed, making them a long-lived shrub. A general application of fertilizer is used in early spring. 'Snowmound' can be found at local nurseries in 2-gallon containers on up to 4' balled and burlapped specimens.

'Snowmound' can be used in many ways. Its compact size makes it ideal for even the smallest gardens. It sits well among conifers, each complementing the other: the conifers' green background shows off the white blossoms of the spirea, while the spirea offers a shorter anchor to lower the scale. It makes a handsome 5' hedge; or use a pair to frame an entrance. This white beauty can divide long swaths of perennials, create height and texture relief, soften and anchor structural features such as fences and walls. And every air conditioning unit sold should come with a 'Snowmound' spirea to hide it from view!

Spiraea x nipponica
'Snowmound'
(spi-re'-a nip-pon'-i-ka)
SNOWMOUND SPIREA

A delicate spirea like 'Ogon Mellow Yellow' can brighten any garden. It is seen here with purple phlox and orange daylily.

This is the best yellow shrub I have ever used, with a graceful openness characterized by arching branches and delicate leaves. It is blessed with bright foliage like its cousin 'Goldmound', but not cursed with pink flowers. Not as readily available as most other spireas, it is worth seeking out.

'Ogon Mellow Yellow' forms a loose, open mound of about 5' x 6'. It is a fast grower and its graceful character begins showing in about two years. Pruning can be accomplished any time after flowering to reshape and encourage new growth. The photograph shows a four-year-old plant that has not as yet been pruned.

Blossoms begin emerging in tight clumps before the leaves come out, on rich dark, reddish-brown stems that are a perfect foil for the pure white flowers. The blossoms run the full length of each branch, along the top side. It is usually the first spirea to flower in April. When the leaves do emerge they are bright yellow and stay deep golden-yellow all season.

'Ogon Mellow Yellow' has proven to be as hardy and vigorous into Zone 4 as other spireas. Moist soil and plenty of sun are requirements for good healthy plants. I have never had any problems with this spirea; if it sails through the winter of 2000 the way I think it will, I will sing its praises even more.

Use 'Mellow Yellow' to brighten and highlight any sunny spot in the garden. It glows with healthy exuberance among green shrubs. It is a good companion for 'Snowmound' spirea, complementing the latter's blue foliage. It blends well with all warm-color perennials such as purple phlox and orange daylilies. I have planted one with a redbud in order to have magenta blossoms floating above the wispy yellow branches of 'Mellow Yellow'. It would also be good with the big leaves of hydrangea for textural contrast.

Spiraea thunbergii
(spi-re'-a thun-ber'-je-i)
'Ogon Mellow Yellow'

Good hedge material, and friendly with perennials and other shrubs, Meyer lilac is versatile in the landscape. It and its dwarf form, 'Palibin', bloom with lilac-pink flowers in late April to early May.

These are hands down the best and the easiest lilacs for the Midwest. True, they do not rival the *S. vulgaris* hybrids for size and fragrance. But beautiful as the common lilacs are, each summer powdery mildew turns them into an unsightly mess. We are told that a fungicide will alleviate the problem, but it is not true, and moreover, spraying is extra work. When I learned about *Syringa meyeri* and its dwarf form, 'Palibin', I was freed of one more "spraying solution."

S. meyeri and *S. m.* 'Palibin' have dense branching with uniform structure that creates an excellent shrub with round form. Both have small dark green leaves that are distinctively wavy at the margins. The former attains a height of 6 to 8', while the latter becomes 4 to 5'. Both can spread to a width one and one-half times their height. They are tidy shrubs whose thick branches and petite foliage hold a good shape during the season. Their versatility makes them indispensable.

The flowers are not as large as common lilacs', but the 4" long clusters more than compensate for size by smothering the entire plant. There is a good lilac fragrance, all the more distinct if cut and taken indoors. The blossoms are said to be susceptible to late freezes, but I have not lived one spring without any blossoms since I began using them fifteen years ago.

Hardy to Zone 3, they require no maintenance unless crowding makes pruning necessary. If initially given proper spacing, there will be nothing to do but water occasionally. Either will bloom more abundantly in full sun, but I have seen them doing quite well under trees. Their tolerance for light shade and for northeast-facing locations is admirable. I have had them in the best of soils as well as in clay, both with success. Prune the spent blossom heads to keep the plant from expending energy producing seed.

Both make good hedges, the Meyer lilac taller and 'Palibin' shorter. I use them around terraces and patios where their prolific bloom and fragrance can be appreciated. 'Palibin' is better for urns because it is smaller, but there is no reason Meyer lilac would not work if the urn was large enough. The Meyer is tall enough to make a good background for peonies, hardy geraniums, and a host of other perennials. Pink, purple and white plants of any kind work well to bloom along with the lilacs. Try a purple-leaved barberry as a companion, along with *Geranium sanguineum* and *Ajuga reptans*. 'Palibin' is effective grouped either with two taxus (e.g., 'Densiformis' or 'Andersonii') and one lilac, or two lilac and one taxus. Such an arrangement has a natural balance and presence, whether standing alone or anchoring a tree or wall.

Syringa meyeri and S. m. 'Palibin'
(si-ring'-guh mi-er-i)
MEYER LILAC,
PALIBIN LILAC

The standard lilac 'Palibin' delivers sweet greetings to visitors at this entrance. Transformed by its striking short trunk, the standard 'Palibin' is even more distinctive and appealing than the shrub form.

The same shrub in an altered form, the standard 'Palibin' produces a completely different effect. If I had included it in the previous essay, there would not be sufficient space to do it justice. To see a photograph of the standard form will erase the abstraction and, I hope, stimulate you to find and use it.

Standard forms of 'Palibin' come grafted to 3–5' trunks, their branches forming an oval-round top. They won't look like much when first planted, but given three years the head will expand and thicken into a nice crown. As the head enlarges it can be pruned into any shape desired. It is a slow grower but worth the wait, for it gets better every year. The head has the capability of becoming 7' wide, but if kept trained to a 4' to 5' spread above the trunk, it will reduce weight on the grafted area and ensure a more stable plant.

Standard 'Palibin' has the same pinkish-purple flowers as *S. meyeri*, but in topiary-tree form. If the shape of the topiary is to be kept tightly branched, it should be pruned hard after it blooms. Otherwise, full sun and good drainage are basic requirements, but like the shrub form it is adaptable to less sun and to most types of soil. Both possess the same hardiness and ease of care. Both transplant easily and can be found in 2- to 5-gallon containers.

Like a miniature tree, a standard 'Palibin' adds immediate height and structure to a planting. Structure is the most conspicuous design feature missing in gardens I am called in to help with. The idea of structure in gardens has unfortunately become synonymous with formality. But structure need not be formal. It does have to be supportive without being the main attraction, like the plot of a story, which holds all the words and meaning together without being the main focus, giving definition and integrated wholeness. That is the reason for using any form of standard.

The various heights that are available can be used for different effects, to accentuate and dramatize an entrance or corner of a building or be placed alone as a focal point. One on either side of an entryway will direct the focus to the steps and lead visitors to the walk. Soon they will grow tall enough to soften and anchor a building's corner by connecting the plantings to the structure. Immediate height can be added to a planting of perennials and shrubs. I have used it with pink tree peonies, early blooming herbaceous peonies, and purple-foliage coralbells. It becomes an instant topiary.

Syringa meyeri
'Palibin' Standard
PALIBIN STANDARD LILAC

A good specimen of Japanese tree lilac. Here, companions of azaleas, pyracantha, and white daylilies are shown. I would throw out everything but the daylilies, replacing the other shrubs with white buddleias to anchor the trees, and adding more all-white daylilies to bloom with the tree lilac.

The Japanese tree lilac is one of the few trees under 35' that has exquisite blossoms late in the season, and its interesting bark adds luster to a drab winter. It should be more widely used. Like the previous two lilacs, it is disease free and culturally undemanding. It is a perfect small tree for the garden, with the added benefits of scented, lilac-type flowers and a rugged constitution.

Syringa reticulata becomes 20–30' tall and 15–25' wide, with a rounded crown. The tree is attractive year-round with its reddish-brown, mahogany bark marked with silvery lenticels like that of a cherry tree and a hardiness to Zone 3. It develops elegant, arching branches with age. I prefer to remove the lower ones and shape it more like a tree, rather than leave it in its bushy shrub form. Hybrids like 'Ivory Silk' and 'Regent' tend to come as single-trunk specimens, while *S. reticulata* is usually found in the nurseries in clump form.

Blossoms are huge clusters of 12", ivory-white flowers beginning in June, when most trees have long finished flowering. Continuing for about two weeks, the blossom clusters spread 10" wide and are fragrant. The leaves are large, dark green, and ovate, with the typical lilac vein reticulation running along the surface. Their underside is tinted grayish-green and is slightly pubescent. As the blossoms deteriorate they turn brown and can be unsightly, but, having more than enough to do, I never bother removing them.

Japanese tree lilac is easy to grow and care for. It prefers well drained and slightly acidic soil but will tolerate clay and has adapted to the sweeter soils here in the Bluegrass area. Although it performs best in cool-summer areas, it flourishes in the Midwest with only occasional leaf burn in the hottest months of summer. Flowering is best in full sun, but an eastern or western facing situation can also be used with confidence. In early spring I remove extraneous inside branches on either the single-trunk or multiple-trunk varieties as well as basal suckers, if any. The crown can be shaped after it flowers, if necessary. I fertilize with a balanced tree-food spike in the late fall or early winter.

Tree lilac is one of the three lilacs I depend upon for hardiness, versatility, and easy care. Small enough to be used in many situations, it is especially effective under a balcony or second-floor window, where it can bloom at eye level. Limb up the lower branches so that light can reach companion plantings below. I was pleased to see them planted in large numbers as street trees in the Clifton area of Cincinnati. Used in large median plantings, they will provide unlimited attraction for the community.

Syringa reticulata
(si-ring'guh re-tik-u-lay'-tuh)
JAPANESE TREE LILAC

The rock-hugging 'Densiformis'
taxus is combined here with a
white azalea and a crabapple.

Yews or taxus are some of the hardiest landscape plants for the North American continent. They will thrive in just about any type of soil, in full sun or shade. They shrug off the hot summers and freezing, wet winters of the Midwest. The only situation that they will not tolerate is standing in wet soil. They are hardy, virtually indestructible, evergreen—and some of the most overused conifers in the country.

Most taxus used for landscaping come from two groups: *Taxus cuspidata* (low, broad, spreading types) and *Taxus x media* (taller, wider types). One of the best pyramidal forms is *T. cuspidata* 'Capitata'. There are round forms from both groups, low spreading types that are used for hedges, and my favorite, the columnar *Taxus* x *media* 'Hicksii' (see below). Yews are highly toxic and should not be used on farms or in the vicinity of livestock and horses. Deer, however, are impervious to this toxicity and can do considerable damage to a hedge of yews if given the opportunity.

T. x media 'Densiformis' is one of the more commonly available and one of the more useful. It can be pruned into a short, flat shrub, wider than tall, or shaped into a broad, oval form. 'Densiformis' can become 3–5' tall x 6–8' wide but is usually pruned into a rectangular hedge or individual squares as foundation plants. It has bright green needles that turn a greenish-brown in winter. *T. x media* 'Andersonii' remains a better green in winter.

An example of 'Densiformis' can be seen in the photograph, its companions a stone and shrubs of azalea and mugo pine, their colors and forms creating a complete arrangement with the nearby crabapple. Another good hybrid for low-spreading hedges would be *T. x m.* 'Wardii', whose mature possibilities are 5–8' by 15–20'.

Uses for 'Deniformis' are endless, although I would like to see fewer of them used in the traditional way, as foundation plantings, mindlessly placed too close to the house. Houses do need anchoring to the landscape but need not be firmly cinched around the foundation.

'Densiformis' has good form to border walks and pathways. It is great to use among other shrubs for color and texture contrast. Like all yews, it can be and has been shaped into just about any form imaginable. One of the best ways to think of taxus is as building blocks—structural material. Forming spaces into rooms, either square or round, is easy with 'Densiformis'. Joining taxus to other plants as shown in the photograph creates an island planting of great beauty anywhere there is space.

Taxus x media
'Densiformis'
(taks'-us me'-di-ah)
ENGLISH-JAPANESE YEW

Taller *Taxus* 'Hicksii' is used here as a green wall to set off daylilies and ornamental grasses.

Taller plant materials that are easily controlled are few in number. The height of the columnar yew can serve many purposes. Its architectural structure can be used to advantage in various ways to connect a building to the garden. *Taxus x media* 'Hicksii' can be kept as a tall, narrow, columnar shrub for smaller gardens or be allowed to mature into a massive wall that is taller than wide. Although a slow grower, it is constant and reliable.

The columnar 'Hicksii' can attain 20' in height and spread 6' or more in width. 'Dynasty' will attain 30'. Bright green needles grow on upright branches that are easily pruned for a narrow space in a smaller garden or left alone to approach mature size in a larger one. Pruning is usually required twice yearly to keep taxus in tight formation. Let it grow naturally, unpruned, as a screen and hedge if there is space and if a less formal style is called for.

Drainage is the most important cultural requirement for 'Hicksii'. Given adequate drainage, it will tolerate most soil types and light situations, including dry shade. Full sun promotes the thickest growth, but taxus will grow in more shade than most plants can handle. It tends to be more open there, but will still provide an all-important structural component. After all, shade is a situation most gardeners have. Overall, it is a most undemanding shrub.

As with all taxus, 'Hicksii' shapes and controls the space but remains in the background, as can be seen in the photo. It makes a excellent tall hedge for separating a garden from other living spaces as well as for dividing rooms inside the garden. 'Hicksii' is tall enough to screen undesired elements around buildings, such as air conditioning units and electric meters that are usually placed at eye level on a wall. Because of its height it can be used as green wall extensions, creating living buttresses and blending structures into the garden. Placed strategically along buildings or walls, it can emphasize a vertical feature or separate sections of space for a pleasing boundary. As a barrier or hedge, 'Hicksii' is one of the best shrubs available, and almost indestructible.

Taxus x media
'Hicksii'
(taks'-us me'-di-ah)
HICKSII YEW

Lacebark elm oversees the
beautiful garden of Betsy and
Louis Hillenmeyer.

An upright tree reminiscent of the elegant American Elm, with fine foliage, decorative, mottled bark, and resistance to Dutch elm disease, Lacebark Elm is graceful, hardy, and undemanding. It is highly versatile for varied soil types and soil pH. Usually a medium-sized tree that can attain 40 to 50' in height and width, it has beautiful, uniform branching, a vase shape, and fine-textured, leathery foliage that matures into a rounded canopy of arching branches. The one drawback of the species is lack of consistency as to size. As Dirr cautions us, at maturity a seedling can be bonsai-sized, or it can be 70' tall. The remedy is to plant one of the new cultivars. 'Allée', 'Athena', and others all have characteristic shapes but grow true to size. Both *Ulmus parvifolia* and the vastly inferior *Ulmus pumila* are sometimes referred to as Chinese Elm, which can be confusing. This is one of those instances when knowing the Latin name can save you from making an expensive mistake. Do not under any circumstances plant *pumila*!

Lacebark Elm has achieved prestige for its wonderful exfoliating bark. Tree trunk and branches display a dappled puzzle of brown, orange, gray, and green that is especially lovely in winter. Trees should be selected for the best bark display because it can vary greatly. Leaves are dark green and serrated at the leaf margins. In a good season, visual appeal is heightened by yellow fall foliage that is lightly brushed with burgundy on the upper surface.

Trees perform their best in well drained, moist and fertile soil, but they are adaptable to the extremes of urban areas and to excessive heat and cold, as well as to different pH levels. In *Trees for Urban and Suburban Landscapes*, Gilman states that lacebark elm is "suitable for street tree pits, parking lot islands, and other confined soil spaces." I have only seen ice damage it once in my area, and then no more so than any other tree, even the mighty oak.

This tree is highly desirable for its year-round visual interest and grow-anywhere fortitude. It can be limbed up as you see in the photograph, allowing other shrubs and perennials to thrive underneath. Or it can be employed as a shade tree by the patio or deck. The bark alone creates a visual feast wherever one chooses to plant it. One on either side of the driveway or front walk entrance will give a dramatic welcome. If you have room for only one tree, the lacebark elm should be seriously considered.

Ulmus parvifolia
(ul'-mus par-vi-foh'-li-ah)
LACEBARK ELM

Viburnum carlesi with Meyer lilac and Japanese maple
'Bloodgood' along a path at the Missouri Botanical Garden.

Viburnums

hen challenged with a difficult situation, I invariably think, and smell, viburnums. When I'm confronted with bad soils, shady areas, hot and dry climates—one of the viburnums will usually work. When I want to enhance an entrance with fragrance, many viburnums come to mind. There are also viburnums valued for their usefulness like *V. dentatum* (arrowwood), while others are known for their ornamental character, such as the doublefile viburnum, and others still for their brilliant fall color, like *V. x burkwoodii* 'Mohawk'.

Flowers range from large globes (*V. x carlcephalum*) to flat clusters of sterile flowers, and flat clusters of smaller flowers orbited by larger sterile flowers (*V. plicatum* var. *tomentosum*). There is a wide range of leaf texture, from long, deeply embossed leatherleaf (*rhytidophyllum*) to velvet-soft *V. carlesii*. The leatherleaf viburnum holds its leaves all year in the Lower Midwest. *VV. opulus* and *trilobum* have maple-shaped leaves. Some viburnums are decorative with attractive berry display, like *V. dilatatum* and its cultivars 'Iroquois' and 'Oneida'. The native arrowwood (*V. dentatum*) has white blossoms, blue berries, and makes an excellent trouble-free hedge or screen.

Sizes range from the 18–24" *Viburnum opulus* 'Nanum' to 30' giants like *V. lentago*, the nannyberry. *V. plicatum*, the Japanese snowball viburnum, has upright growth, contrasted with *V. plicatum tomentosum* 'Mariesii' with distinctive horizontal branching. There are many that are practical for smaller places, such as 4–5' tall *V. utile* 'Eskimo'. One of my current favorites, blooming later than most other viburnums in June, is *V. nudum* 'Winterthur'.

All viburnums I have used show vigorous growing habits, some to a greater extent than one would like when not given adequate space. This vigor allows them to tolerate a variety of soils beyond the "ideal," and a little more shade than usually suggested. Of course, under such conditions one cannot expect great abundance of foliage and flower, but by expecting less than perfection, while pushing cultural requirements, viburnums can serve well in some problem areas as they enhance any mixed shrub, conifer, or perennial border with all-season interest, with the added bonus of being excellent for birds. Midwestern gardeners should collect as many of this large family of shrubs as they have space for.

Used in a mixed border of trees and shrubs, the white blooming Koreanspice viburnum is at its best. Seen here with azaleas, barberries, and pine.

Inclusion of *Viburnum carlesii* is my way of honoring an old standby and at the same time introducing some of the newer hybrids that are now available in nurseries. Without *V. carlesii,* the world of fragrant viburnums would be less to nonexistent. There are more reliable hybrids like *V.* x *juddii* (Zones 4–8) that will cause it to be grown less, but I hope *carlesii* is never totally taken out of production. I think the example in the photograph proves it remains an interesting shrub.

Koreanspice can become 4 to 8' tall and wide—possibly larger—while the Judd viburnum is a full, rounded shrub and 6 to 8'. Thick branches spread upward forming a loosely rounded outline, with velvety, ovate leaves that will turn a bright orange-red in the fall, given the proper seasonal stimulation. 'Aurora' is 6 x 8' tall and wide, while 'Cayuga' should become 6' x 6' in the Lower Midwest.

V. carlesii is known for its heavenly scented 3" blossom clusters consisting of individual flowers that are reddish-pink in bud, opening white. 'Aurora' has larger 5" blossom clusters that open a pinkish-white. The clusters are rounded and can be seen covering the plant in the accompanying photograph. In late April flowers set above flat-green, velvety foliage are in full bloom, and continue into May. Fall foliage can turn a bright dark red to reddish-purple. *V.* x *juddii* blooms earlier, April to May.

Koreanspice prefers well drained, slightly acidic soil that holds even moisture, either in full sun or part shade. Associated with trees in direct sun, under their canopy, and in an eastern facing site are all examples of part shade. Koreanspice is not as easy to grow as Judd viburnum and is more susceptible to leaf spot and less adaptable than either Burkwood or Judd. Nevertheless, it is easily transplanted from container or balled and burlapped. All three are hardy for the Midwest.

Plant Koreanspice to take advantage of its clove-like fragrance when in bloom. The best possible placement is next to a walk or entrance. Cut branches and take inside as often as you can while the blossoms are available. It is good to plant among other trees and shrubs and can be kept pruned to just about any size desired. The group photograph shows it sharing space with companions of Scotch pine (*Pinus silvestris*), barberry, quince, and shrub euonymus at the Missouri Botanical Garden.

Viburnum carlesii
(vi-ber'-num kar-le'se-i)
KOREANSPICE VIBURNUM

Lighting from above
highlights the layering
effect of doublefile
viburnum.

A most elegant shrub with graceful horizontal branching that deserves the highest praise for its large flowers as well as its fruit. Its stratified layering is unique among shrubs and gives the same effect that mature dogwoods do. Blossoms seemingly float above the branches on raised stems, arranged in two rows.

Plants can reach 8 to 10' tall by 9 to 12' wide, with larger plants reported. The one in the photograph is taller than it is wide, about 9' x 7', because the width has been pruned. Leaves are deeply engraved with veins that run from pale-red midrib out to the serrated edge with the same red brushed along the margin. Large white outer flowers orbit an inner constellation of smaller flowers, both totaling 6" across. The blossoms extend upward on their stems, spreading flat above the foliage as they mature in April and May. The small, egg-shaped fruits can make a beautiful bright red display in the fall if the birds don't get to them first.

Culture is not demanding if good drainage and full sun are available, because doublefile viburnum is hardy and disease free. Moist soil should be the gardener's first consideration when locating this viburnum. It has fibrous roots, close to the surface, that require constant moisture and do not tolerate clay soils well. Mulch helps with moisture retention, but if the site does not drain well, I would choose another shrub for the job. It is a good choice for a partly shady position and under a tree where it can receive bright light but not direct sun. If stem dieback occurs, cut down to well past the infection and throw away. Old shrubs can be rejuvenated by cutting them down to a foot of stem.

Doublefile is best displayed when planted against a background of dark green conifers, blue spruce, or a dark brick building. However, the one shown in the photograph has none of the above-suggested background and still looks great. Companions could be *Weigela* 'Park Princess' (a lovely pink), *Picea pungens* 'Hoopsii', and *Syringa meyeri*. Good complementary trees would be 'Bloodgood' Japanese maple, lacebark elm, redbud, and pink dogwood. A long, continuous planting of doublefile viburnum would screen any unwanted view, where there is room for it to spread.

Viburnum plicatum var. *tomentosum*
(vi-ber'-num pli-ka'-tum to-men-to'-sum)
DOUBLEFILE VIBURNUM

The floriferous viburnum
'Eskimo' brightens the
path at the University of
Kentucky Arboretum.

This might just be the perfect viburnum. Take the native *Viburnum utile* and cross it with *V. carlcephalum* 'Cayuga' and you end up with a short, floriferous shrub that is almost too good to be true, except that it is not fragrant. Retaining the best attributes of its parents and adding some wonderful improvements, this relatively new viburnum was released by the U.S. National Arboretum in the early 1980s and is a 2001 Theodore Klein Plant Award Winner. It tends to bloom late for a viburnum, making it an important asset to prolonged showtime in the garden, and its compact size makes it more companionable in a mixed planting than, say, the Burkwood. It has creamy buds that turn into pure white little snowballs. You can hardly see the plant in the photograph for the thick cover of blossoms.

Spreading about 5 x 5', 'Eskimo' is an important shrub for Zones 6–8 and will do fine in Zone 5 too, with a little protection from winter sun and wind. Like any viburnum, it takes readily to pruning. These viburnums are especially rewarding because they are attractive, compact, and ideal for the smaller garden.

The blossoms of 'Eskimo' begin as creamy buds, flushed with soft pink, in late April. In May, they open into 4" snowballs formed of miniature white trumpets, each tiny floret displaying the typical five-petaled viburnum structure. Yellow stamens show in the center. Each cluster has 80 to 175 florets. Cut long sprays to arrange with daffodils or tulips for wonderful indoor arrangements. Dull red fruits develop in August and later turn black in the fall, if they last until then.

With no serious threat of insects or disease, 'Eskimo' is self-sufficient in full or part sun. Well-drained soil should be a consideration, as with any viburnum. It prefers heavy loam and a pH of 6.0–6.5, but I have had acceptable performance in sweeter, clay soil. It is heat tolerant in our grueling summers. Plants can be found in 3- and 5-gallon pots and as larger B&B plants.

The 'Eskimo' in the photo is along the outer path at the U.K. Arboretum. Its overwhelming abundance of blossom always comes as a surprise when I turn the corner and happen upon it. It is sandwiched among other viburnums: 'Allegheny' in the background, the June-blooming 'Winterthur' on the right, and, unseen, *burkwoodii* on the left.

'Eskimo' goes well with a selection of blue, green, and yellow conifers, such as spruce, taxus, and Japanese falsecypress. It is extremely effective planted at an entrance. It is a great shrub for the perennial border, and makes a striking hedge.

Viburnum utile
'Eskimo'
(vi-ber'-num u'ti-lee)
SERVICE VIBURNUM

Weigela 'Park Princess' is a soft companion with white peonies.

Since its introduction in 1845 from temperate eastern Asia, this tubular-flowered beauty has impressed gardeners all over the world with its pink blossoms and pollution tolerance. *Weigela florida* and its cultivars are also highly adaptable and have no major disease or insect problems. In flower, they look great; when not in bloom, they need to be obscured by other shrubs.

Densely spreading to become 6 to 9' tall, 'Park Princess' can extend 6 to 8' wide with branches that hang to the ground. There are many other cultivars of all sizes, including 'Minuet' at 30" x 3', 'Rumba' at 3' x 3', and 'White Knight' at 5' x 5', hardy in Zones 5-8.

The flowers are elongated, tubular extensions ending in a five-lobed trumpet. Buds are dark pink when they first open, fading to a wonderful clear pink as they mature. Blossoms emerge on last year's branches with short stems holding single or multiple flowers in May to June. There are two weigelas in the photograph, both planted as 'Park Princess'. As it turned out, one was a red variety. Nevertheless, they have served the situation well over twelve years. Most weigelas' foliage is a medium green, but there are attractive variegated-foliage types, all with rosy-pink flowers.

Weigelas are easily grown in urban gardens and public places because of their pollution tolerance. They do their best in full sun and well-drained soil but will tolerate slightly less light, resulting in fewer blossoms and more open branching. Branch dieback will occur, but a good pruning after flowering will rejuvenate the shrub for the next season. Nurseries usually carry weigelas in containers and sometimes larger balled and burlapped specimens.

Where there is space, weigelas are best viewed from a distance, planted with other shrubs to redirect visual attention after blossoms fade and where their coarse branches will not have a prime location during the winter months. They are good companions for peonies—white 'Festiva Maxima' is seen in the photograph. Weigela 'White Knight' is a good component of an all-white garden and looks pretty planted near swimming and ornamental pools to soften and reflect in the water.

Weigela florida
'Park Princess'
(wi-ge'-la flor'-i-da)
OLD-FASHIONED WEIGELA

Resources

Nurseries (Mail Order and Otherwise)

Altums Horticultural Center and Gardens, 11335 N. Michigan Road, Zionsville, IN 46077. (317) 733-4769. Trees and shrubs.

Ammon Wholesale Nursery, 6089 Camp Ernst Road, Burlington, KY 41005. (800) 972-3406. Trees, shrubs, and roses. To the trade only.

The Antique Rose Emporium, 9300 Lueckemeyer Road, Brenham, TX 77833. (800) 441-0002. Mail order. Roses.

Arborvillage, 15604 County Road "CC," P.O. Box 227, Holt, MO 64048. (816) 264-3911. Mail order. Trees and shrubs.

Baker's Village Garden Center, 9267 Dublin Road, Powell, OH 43065. (614) 889-9407. Trees, shrubs, and roses.

Beaver Creek Nursery, 6604 Randall Road, Poplar Grove, IL 61065-9005. (815) 737-8758. Container grown and B&B trees and shrubs. To the trade only.

Brehob Nursery, Inc., 4316 Bluff Road, Indianapolis, IN 46217. (800) 921-3233. Container grown and B&B trees and shrubs. To the trade only.

Briggsville Gardens, 3273 Mathey Road, Sturgeon Bay, WI 54235. (920) 743-1246. Specialty trees and shrubs.

Burnham Woods Nursery, 6775 Hudoff Road, Bloomington, IN 47408. (812) 339-0616. Flowering shrubs, including newer dwarf forms that combine well with perennials.

J. Carlson Growers Nursery, 8938 Newburg Road, Rockford, IL 61108. (815) 332-5610. Trees, especially Asian, also rhododendrons.

Carroll Gardens, 44 E. Main St., Westminster, MD 21158. (800) 876-7336. Mail order. Lilacs, mockorange.

Chalet Nursery, 3132 Lake Avenue, Wilmette, IL 60091. (847) 256-0561. Trees, shrubs, including rhododendrons, and roses.

Chamblee's Rose Nursery, 10926 U.S. Highway 69N, Tyler, TX 75706. (800) 256-7673. Mail order. Roses.

Dannaher Landscaping, 12200 Vans Valley Road, Galena, OH 43021. (740) 965-3789. Deciduous trees including unique magnolias; conifers; shrubs including witchhazels. By appointment.

Dintelmann's Nursery, 1720 Centerville Avenue, Belleville, IL 62220. (618) 233-4638. Trees and shrubs.

Enchanted Valley Gardens, 9123 N. Territorial Road, Evansville, WI 53536. (608) 882-4200. Trees and shrubs.

The Essentially English Garden, 6599 US Route 35 East, Jamestown, OH 45335. (937) 675-7055. Rare and unusual trees and shrubs.

Evergreen Nursery Co., Inc., 5027 County Trunk TT, Sturgeon Bay, WI 54235. (800) 448-5691; (920) 743-4464. To the trade only.

Fairweather Gardens, P. O. Box 330, Greenwich, NJ 08323. (609) 451-6261. Mail order. Trees and shrubs.

C. J. Fiore Co., 16606 W. Highway 22, Prairie View, IL 60069. (847) 913-1414. Trees and shrubs. Wholesale and retail.

Forestfarm, 990 Tetherow Road, Williams, OR 97544. (541) 846-7269. Mail order. Trees and shrubs.

Forrest Keeling Nursery, P.O. Box 135, Elsberry, MO 63343. (800) 356-2401. Deciduous trees and shrubs, some native.

Fox Hill Nursery, 347 Lunt Road, Freeport, ME 04032. (207) 729-1511. Mail order. Lilacs.

Gee Farms, 14928 Bunkerhill Road, Stockbridge, MI 49285. (800) 860-BUSH or (517) 769-6772. Trees, shrubs, conifers. Also mail order.

Geimer Greenhouses, Inc., 701 E. Dundee Road, Arlington Heights, IL 60004. (847) 259-6363. Trees and shrubs.

The Greenery, 1021 West Delmar, Godfrey, IL 62035. (618) 466-8475. Trees and shrubs.

The Growing Place, Plank Road, Naperville, IL 60563. (630) 355-4000, and Montgomery Road, Aurora, IL 60504. (630) 820-8088. Trees and shrubs, including spireas, viburnums.

Heirloom Roses, 24062 N.E. Riverside Drive, St. Paul, OR 97137. (503) 538-1576. Mail order. Roses.

Hermsen Nursery, 11463 Jamesmeier Road, Farley, IA 52046. (319) 744-3991. Rare, dwarf, and unusual conifers.

Heronswood Nursery, Ltd. 7530 N.E. 288th Street, Kingston, WA 98346. (360) 297-4172. Mail order. Trees and shrubs.

Hillenmeyer Nursery, 2370 Sandersville Road, Lexington, KY 40511. (859) 255-1091. Trees, shrubs, and roses.

Holly Hills, 1216 E. Hillsdale Road, Evansville, IN 47725-1217. (812) 867-3367. Hollies.

Kentucky Wholesale Nursery, Winchester, KY 40391. (606) 745-5343. Trees and shrubs. To the trade only.

Kirkwood Gardens, 2701 Barrett Station Road, St. Louis, MO 63021. (314) 966-3343. Trees and shrubs.

Lakeview Garden Center, 6061 Pleasant Avenue, Fairfield, OH 45014. (513) 829-6624. Deciduous trees and conifers of all sizes, shrubs, and roses.

The Landscape Supply, 2435 Burlington Pike, Burlington, KY 41005. (606) 586-5200. Trees, shrubs, and roses.

Lowe's Own-root Roses, 6 Sheffield Road, Nashua, NH 03062. (603) 888-2214. Mail order. Roses.

Mellinger's Nursery, 2310 W. South Range Road, North Lima, OH 44452. (800) 321-7444. Mail order. Hollies, other shrubs.

Michler Greenhouses, 417 E. Maxwell Street, Lexington, KY 40508. (859) 254-0383. Trees, shrubs, and roses.

Miller's Manor Gardens, 12788 E. 191st Street, Noblesville, IN 46060. (317) 770-7678. Hard to find dwarf conifers. Ornamental trees and shrubs.

Passiglia's Nursery and Garden Center, 1855 Highway 109, Glencoe, MO 63038. (636) 458-9202. Trees and shrubs.

Pickering Nurseries, Inc., 670 Kingston Road, Pickering, Ontario L1V 1A6. (905) 839-2111. Mail order. Roses.

The Plant Kingdom, 4101 Westport Road, Louisville, KY 40207. (502) 893-7333. Trees and shrubs, including natives.

Rahn's Greenhouse, 4944 Gray Road, Cincinnati, OH 45232. (513) 541-0672. Shrubs and roses.

Rich's Foxwillow Pines, 11618 McConnell Road, Woodstock, IL 60098. (815) 338-7442. Conifers, trees.

Ridge Road Nursery, 3195 St. Catherine Road, Bellevue, IA 52031. (319) 583-1381. Woody ornamentals, including unusual viburnums.

Sargents Landscape Nursery, 7955 18th Avenue NW, Rochester, MN 55901. (507) 289-0022. Trees and shrubs.

Schmid Nursery and Gardens, 847 Westwood Boulevard, Jackson, MI 49203. (517) 787-5275. Shrubs, trees, and conifers, particularly rare and dwarf varieties.

Schmittle's Nursery, 3406 Creve Coeur Mill Road. Creve Coeur, MO 63146. (314) 469-8900. Trees and shrubs.

Sherwood's Forest Nursery and Garden Center, 2651 Barrett Station Road, St. Louis, MO 60302. (314) 966-0028. Trees and shrubs.

Sid's Nursery, 10926 Southwest Highway, Palos Hills, IL 60465. (708) 974-4500. Trees, shrubs, roses.

Simpson Nursery Co., 1504 Wheatland Road, P O Box 2065, Vincennes, IN 47591. Hollies. To the trade only.

Singer Gardens, 2316 Stamping Ground Road, Stamping Ground, KY 40379. (502) 535-6222. Trees and shrubs.

Skaggs Enterprises Inc., 4101 W. Thompson Road, Indianapolis, IN 46221. (317) 856-7397. Trees and shrubs.

Spring Bluff Nursery, 41 W 130 Norris Road, Sugar Grove, IL 60554. (630) 466-4278. Trees and shrubs, including azaleas, ilex, spireas.

Springhouse Gardens, 6041 Harrodsburg Road, Nicholasville, KY 40356. (859) 224-1417. Trees and shrubs.

Timber Creek Nursery, 54 Clarkson Road. Ellisville, MO 63011. (636) 227-0095. Trees and shrubs.

Treeland Nursery, 615 Old State Road, Glencoe, MO 63038. (636) 391-3909. Trees, shrubs, and evergreens.

A. Waldbart & Sons Nursery, 5517 N Highway 67, St. Louis, MO 63034. (314) 741-3121. Trees and shrubs.

Wallitsch Nursery and Garden Center, 2608 Hikes Lane, Louisville, KY 40218. (502) 454-3553.

Wavecrest Nursery, 2509 Lakeshore Drive, Fennville, MI 49408. (616) 543-4175. Deciduous and evergreen trees and shrubs.

We-Du Nurseries, Route 5, Box 724, Marion, NC 28752. (828) 738-8300. Mail order. Trees and shrubs.

White Flower Farm, P.O. Box 50, Litchfield, CT 06759. (800) 503-9624. Mail order. Selected trees and shrubs.

Books

David Austin, *The Heritage of The Rose*. Woodbridge, Suffolk: Antique Collector's Club, Ltd., 1988.

Peter Beales, *Classic Roses*. New York: Henry Holt, 1985.

George E. Brown, *The Pruning of Trees, Shrubs, and Conifers*. Portland, OR: Timber Press, 1995.

Tom Christopher, *Easy Roses for North American Gardens*. Pleasantville, NY: Reader's Digest, 1999.

Michael A. Dirr, *Dirr's Hardy Trees and Shrubs: An Illustrated Encyclopedia* (Portland, OR.: Timber Press, 1997)

Michael A. Dirr, *Manual of Woody Landscape Plants*. Champaign, IL: Stipes Publishing, 1998.

Fred C. Galle, *Hollies: The Genus Ilex*. Portland, OR: Timber Press, 1997.

Garden Club of America, Janet Meakin Poor, Nancy P. Brewster, *Plants That Merit Attention, Vol. 2, Shrubs*. Portland, OR: Timber Press, 1997.

Galen Gates, Ethan Johnson, Ruth Rodgers, The Holden Arboretum, and Chicago Botanic Garden, *Trees* (American Garden Guides). New York: Pantheon Books, 1996.

S. Millar Gault and Patrick M. Synge, *The Dictionary of Roses in Color*. London: Mermaid Books, 1971.

Edward F. Gilman, *Trees for Urban and Suburban Landscapes*. Albany, NY: Delmar, 1997.

Harold E. Greer, *Greer's Guidebook to Available Rhododendrons*. Eugene, OR: Offshoot Publications, 1988.

Diane Heilenman, *Gardening in the Lower Midwest*. Bloomington: Indiana University Press, 1994.

The Hillier Gardener's Guide to Trees and Shrubs. Pleasantville, NY: Reader's Digest, 1997.

Wybe Kuitert, *Japanese Flowering Cherries*. Portland, OR: Timber Press, 1999.

Tim Morehouse with Frank Clark and Ezra Haggard, *Basic Projects and Plantings for the Garden*. Harrisburg, Pa.: Stackpole Books, 1993.

Maggie Oster, *The Rose Book: How to Grow Roses Organically*. Emmaus, PA: Rodale Press, 1994.

Homer E. Salley and Harold E. Greer, *Rhododendron Hybrids: A Guide to Their Origins*. Portland, OR: Timber Press, 1986.

Graham Stuart Thomas, *Trees in the Landscape*. London: Jonathan Cape Ltd. with The National Trust, 1983.

J. D. Vertrees, *Japanese Maples*. Forest Grove, OR: Timber Press, 1978.

Donald Wyman, *Wyman's Gardening Encyclopedia*. New York: Macmillan, 1986.

Index

LANDSCAPE DESIGNER
EZRA HAGGARD
HAS A QUARTER-CENTURY OF
HANDS-ON HORTICULTURAL EXPERIENCE
BUILDING GARDENS IN THE MIDWEST.
HE IS AMPLY QUALIFIED TO ADVISE ON
HOW TO MAKE OUR GARDENS MORE
BEAUTIFUL AND INTERESTING AND OUR
GARDENING LIVES EASIER AND
MORE SATISFYING.
HE IS ALSO AUTHOR AND
PHOTOGRAPHER OF "PERENNIALS
FOR THE LOWER MIDWEST"
(1996).

Editor: *Roberta Diehl*
Sponsoring Editor: *Roberta Diehl*
Book and Jacket designer: *Pamela Rude*
Typefaces: *Berkeley, Trajan*
Printer: *Tien Wah Press PTE LTD*